The City, Seen as a Garden of Ideas
Peter Cook

THE MONACELLI PRESS

To Yael and Alexander, my chirpy family

First published in the United States of America in 2003 by The Monacelli Press, Inc.
902 Broadway, New York, New York 10010

Library of Congress Cataloging-in-Publication Data

Cook, Peter.
  The city, seen as a garden of ideas / Peter Cook.
     p. cm.
  ISBN 1-58093-102-2
  ISBN 1-58093-108-1 (pbk)
  1. City planning--History--20th century. I. Title.
  NA9095.C66 2003
  711'.4--dc22
                              2003015603

Designed by Sze Tsung Leong and Chuihua Judy Chung
Printed and bound in Italy

Contents

INTRODUCTION

I am lucky to be someone who is paid to talk about what I do and what I think about what I do. Also, of course, I am paid to second-guess what other people do. Yet if I am suddenly asked about my activity (on a plane or a train or in a burger bar) I say, "I'm a designer."

Funny that. Perhaps it is a wish-dream. Perhaps it is a conscious reminder-symbol. Perhaps there is more rhetoric to the statement than I am letting on.

Certainly I have a special regard for the architectural critics who were educated as designers or architects: Colin Rowe, Toshio Nakamura, Michael Sorkin, or Kenneth Frampton. Most of all for Reyner Banham (former aircraft engineer), from whom I learned so much. There is surely a series of trains of thought, causes and effects, responses to conditions that come, simply, from designing one's way out of a corner.

Another giveaway. One that you might spot in this book. As "designer" visitors to a new city, as discoverers of a new spot, enthusiasts for the potential of a site, we immediately start to figure out how it could be manipulated. We comment on its qualities (but secretly want to build upon them). We identify the quality and want to take it on board, add it to the rest of the flotsam and jetsam of devices from which we draw.

While this book is ostensibly detached from the process of design, it is devised as a series of references back. In offering clues to what inspires or amuses (and occasionally, what irritates), it is almost hinting at a scale of values.

The ultimate frustration is that no book, film, lecture, animated analysis devised so far can reproduce the real characteristics of space. The true effect of noise, dampness, mustiness, decadence, squeaky-cleanliness, dumbness of the place itself. No means exists to replace the instinctive will to stroke, tap, poke, pick at a wall or a panel.

Meanwhile we draw and write. Too many of my friends who can draw seem to feel that they should write. I wish that they wrote like they drew, but they want to please the writing people.

I want to please the drawing people.

I want to encourage the looking people to become drawing people. The drawing people to keep looking, keep appropriating, and then keep drawing. The writing to act merely as a lubricant.

Do I give too much away?

Peter Cook
London, 2003

THE CITY OF INCIDENTS

Imagine yourself putting together all your favorite memories in an unending and loosely fitting jigsaw in such a way that you could always wander back through them, indulging and enjoying them at will. In such a way that they can be endlessly rearranged or juxtaposed. Ultimately, the effect becomes faintly exotic. The old favorites are tweaked by new playmates, the half-memories overlaid by more recent experiences. Strange new mixtures of fact and fantasy filter through. New—but perhaps only conjectured—memories emerge out of the scrambling process.

Now imagine yourself starting to manipulate these memories and hybrid memories, starting to infiltrate the experienced with the could-be-experienced and, as the adrenaline surges, the might-be-experienced and even beyond: to the if-only-they-could-be-experienced. Dreaming headily through to another world, one that draws upon the real and the reasonable only as it feels the need. Otherwise letting itself drift into the territory that the makers of the first collages in the 1910s, the filmmakers of the 1940s, and innumerable electronic wizards of more recent times must have sensed as they became immured in the combination of technical prowess and drifting imagination.

So I am playing with my memories and responses: I simply cannot make architecture out of thin air, I can hardly bear to make architecture out of the procedural stacking of circumstance upon circumstance, motive upon motive, function upon function and there are many times that I am dissatisfied with a simple search for the "spirit of the site." I am too much a believer in alchemy: in the strange—but nice—sequence of forces that emanates from the sudden, oblique stab at the problem that in its very inexactitude and personality (or perversity?) turns every part of the ensuing chain reaction into a voyage of discovery. Looking back over the "process" of an idea or a design, I am often reduced to wry laughter at the twists and turns: that a piece of architecture thus produced is perfectly responding to an outrageous set of forces, an unlikely set of bedfellows, a quaint family of parts . . . but in a remarkably calm way . . . *all things considered!*

I cannot take architecture out of thin air . . . but certainly enjoy taking it out of thick air!

Searching for thick air as one writes about one's preoccupations is not as difficult as it might seem: all you have to do is to summon up that scrambled and unreliable memory alluded to earlier, then structure it by way of some linked experiences. Couple some of these to places, couple others to projects. Even couple the projects and the places— though this may quickly become artificial, especially if true alchemy is to be involved. Twisting what one sees. Twisting it again into what one *might* see.

Dragon style. Hollmenkollern Hotel, Oslo, 1909.

Oslo: The Building Suddenly Moved

Oslo is a city with a quiet charm: active but unhurried, expansive but not intense. Characterized by the opened curtains and welcoming lights of its living rooms seen in the quiet part of the evening, that period between teatime and the later drinking time. The resulting picture is a mass of books, art on the walls, comfortable contemplation going on somewhere within. Some energetic machine up on a mountain is catching the energy of melted snows: captured so elegantly as to sustain this calm illumination of such little physical movement. A large city in hectares, but most of it lurks among the trees: even the potential substance of the inner city is fragmented into a series of small episodes from the harder cities of Northern Europe that only sustain themselves for two and a half blocks here or two blocks there: a steeple or a quirky tower acting as a marker across five or six shifts of city grain, helped of course by the topography of gentle fingers of rock climbing up out of the Oslo Fjord. You can track the whole history of three or four hundred years of politics, adventure, provincialism, or architectural bandwagoning more easily here than in London, Paris, or Berlin, where the surges of power and enterprise were so much vaster. The final independence of Norway and the reinvention of Christiania first had to be accompanied by the quirky and gestural architecture of the Dragon style, with its chunky obligation to the stave churches and the Viking ships: the Dragon itself became a spookier and more impressive totem as it was chopped out of the timber stave or prow. That this wooden formalism could then be integrated into stone- and iron-based profiles is no more remarkable in its way than the weaving of plants into the same materials in Flanders or Glasgow.

The subsequent attachment to benign socialism and a direct extrapolation of this into Norwegian Funkis architecture can be read through two or three conveniently parallel circumstances. First, the process of urbanization: the sailors and fisherfolk, as well as the isolated valley communities, surged toward the new sources of employment and the comfortable but essentially egalitarian apartment blocks. Second, there was an intelligent craft tradition (that still has the capability to make a hardwood windowsill sing in the twenty-first century), delighting in that same IKEA-logic that we all buy into on a Saturday afternoon: a comfy marriage of the band saw and the high-tensile screw. A 1970s phenomenon, it has roots in 1930s Nordic social rationalization. Add to these a creative detachment from the banners and shrieks of Moscow, Leipzig, or Birmingham . . . with, again, that cheap power, and you have a basis for good, clean, procedural functioning architecture. But with this Funkis we must remember that the Norwegians are said to be the Irish of Scandinavia—with more than a hint of aquavit or blarney in their interpretation. It is neither quite so comfy as Danish nor as dogmatic as the more celebrated Swedish model. The setting can now be added in: a strange turn in the road, a surprising outcrop of ground—even in the middle of a city—plenty of trees to break down the dogma, and never more than a couple of blocks of *anything*.

LAYER CITY, LOCAL PLAN
Streams and "wafts" of plantation run counter to the various
geometries of the building types, such as offices, villas, and so on.

OUTRIDERS OF LAYER CITY
(Peter Cook, 1981)
The towers are based in the Oslo Fjord; layers of inhabited hillside rise up inland.

Layer City was created during my longest stay in Oslo, from mid-August to late December: such a metamorphosis of atmosphere that drives even the more fragile locals to lose themselves in an alcoholic haze or jump straight through the window. They contemplate the gradual disappearance of sun, then of cracks in the clouds, of highlights, of anything except variants of gray. In Finland, November is "mud month." In Oslo it must surely be "gloom month." Paradoxically, the unique subtlety of Funkis (and probably pre-Funkis) coloration comes out of this gray. The mute blue-green, the grayed magenta, the softened purple are legitimate public hues for sensible buildings in that city. In a sense, the more familiar jolly bright yellows and oranges of children's clothes and sunblinds (which also come from the north) are a far coarser and more obvious rejoinder to the deprivation of sunshine. Yet at a certain moment, one responds with a similar knee-jerk coarseness and sets up profiles to the congealed cloud. As they do most energetically in Helsinki, where even the murkiest sky is challenged by the mass of the early-twentieth-century turrets of Lars Sonck and his friends: memory of content through a shadow-puppetry of mute solidity.

The **Outriders of Layer City** were composed in this way and placed in the simplest of settings: surrounded by the waters of the fjord. No problem here, either, since a substantial part of Oslo's commuter population boats its way in from populated islands large and small. Why not place the apex of a city system in the relative tabula rasa of the water? And then, as the layers of hinterland build up, let it spread onto the hillsides, interweave with the waterfalls and rocks, with slivers of built form woven into slivers of pathway, slivers of plantation, slivers of screen, slivers of active interruption. The most interesting part of the drawing became the hint of these slivers that is suggested in the patches between the towers that are themselves a little too amused perhaps by the Dragon-Jugendstil period of Henrik Bull's work. A local hero of some sophistication, Bull could lurch from the Paris-influenced and essentially bourgeois demands of the National Theatre of the 1890s to the lyrical Jugendstil of the Craft Museum and some chunky street corners of the 1920s. This ability to course a city, recognize mannerisms, walk along historical/political shifts in twenty minutes, or detach case histories—an overwhelming task in London or Berlin—was for me a pleasant indulgence in Oslo. Added to which, I have always had a love-hate-love relationship to Jugendstil. (By the way, it's even harder if you use the French term "Art Nouveau" for a kid brought up with a cultural suspicion of those who do "arty" things to architecture—Nouveau or no Nouveau!). But Youth! The *Young* style . . . now that has a good ring to it! I enjoy the fruity pushing and pulling of the mass material. The inevitable absorption of mechanized techniques. The need for wrought and fashioned (i.e., metal) elements to become the culmination of an idea, rather than just the bolts and hinges. Containing the seeds of an industrial architecture: just one or two faltering steps from these major articulations through to the gestures of Gropius and on to Jean Prouvé and the boys.

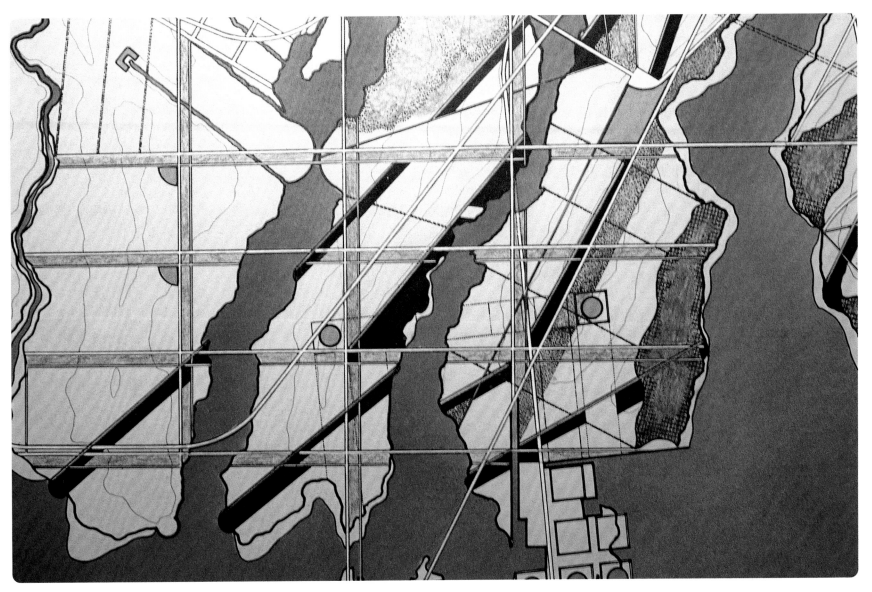

LAYER CITY
Layout of the main routes and identity points. The "outriders" are in the water and are the focus of the city. The local plan adjoins the semicircular identity point.

Holed away in Oslo, I could make a studied detail of Layer City. I could sit there in the same studio as the students of the Oslo School of Architecture and draw my own corner of the hinterland: up on the same set of hills—though Layer City was never suggested as a replacement of Oslo. Rather, it was to be situated to the west, somewhere near Drammen, perhaps. To be inhabited by office workers and their offices, high-tech enterprises, with pavilions in among the trees where you could stroll and work: a quotation, in certain ways, of what has subsequently happened in the Lysaker-Drammen belt. Christine Hawley's Shadow House plan (I myself had made about 10 percent of the design, particularly the "gardened" bits) was appropriated: its water-garden cascading out and down the hillside. More watercourses were added deliberately as slivers. Then an idea about pavilions: office trays borrowed from a 1959 project when, as an AA student, I devised such rotating trays for offices as a way to have continuous open space and gardens with the "sandwich" of the office only occurring on one in four of the layers. These pavilions could tumble down the hill. The gardening from the Shadow House now could really get going: with small geometric shifts. Small networks of "retreat" pavilions—remembered either from the Bergman film *Smiles of a Summer Night* or maybe from the Rousham gardens in Oxfordshire.

Add, too, a series of less geometrically sober "wafts" of space, figuratively akin to the snakes in the board game hoping for the optimism of the ladders. These wafts were my favorite, perhaps created out of childhood memories of Letchworth or adolescent memories of Bournemouth where, in both cases, English provincial folk clad in sensible shoes and undoubtedly of only good intentions were encouraged to perambulate at no particular speed through the backs of the town down a path consistently lined by vegetation—essentially tightly wrapped vegetation but of uneven mass. Picturesque, yet without a *particular* pictorial objective. Allowing for the fact that in my interpretation, all of the sets—gardens, pavilions, watercourses, and the rest—were deliberately jangled together on a variety of geometric shifts and frequently challenging each other. It was the essential nonchalance of the wafts that I enjoyed: strolling through their systematics and occasional discomfiture.

Fjord activity including a ferry ship, Oslo.

One afternoon I stood at the apex of that much-boated patch of water that lies between the main city and Bygdoy—the sweet peninsula of the Summer Palace and the Folk Museum. On my left, among the inevitable trees, were some old villas, small office buildings, and apartments. But toward the end of that strip I could see a decently proportioned white block, six or eight floors high. Despite frequent rides past this spot I was totally surprised by its presence—more irritated with myself that I had not previously spotted a good piece of architecture in this pleasant mix.

Then it moved. For it was the superstructure of the big ship that goes to Keil.

Up to that point my Oslo, my gentle interwoven slopes, my provocative slivers, and my projects for such places were dynamically well behaved. The days of mobile elements were something of a memory: of the hovercraft-as-building in **Plug-in City** or the car-furniture or the **Instant Village**. Scatological in their habits, aggressive even. But the building-that-moved in this gentle, absorptive setting seemed altogether reasonable—no, more than that, it seemed totally *apt.* At which point I am forced to return to a central worry that I have concerning some of the best of Modern architecture: namely, its intellectual and formal tussle with movement and the expression of movement. If I am the child of the machine and forever imagine the task of architecture to be capturing the moment and then creating the opportunity for the next moment, I suffer the paradox. The task is surely to *facilitate* it. Then surely I am talking about an architecture in which technology can help us to flex and respond: it can be an architecture that moves.

Yet I admire those frozen gyrations of the Vesnin brothers, of Konstantin Melnikov, of Zaha Hadid, of Neil Denari, of Coop Himmelblau. To capture the twentieth century in flight—this was the ambition. Yet with a frozen flight-path and a trajectory marked and celebrated but not really trajecting.

That calm afternoon by Bygdoy was the more poignant by way of its contextual gentleness and its inevitability of absorption of the idea of a city that can move—of a collage that can slip in front of your very eyes. I could no longer remain passive about the issue. It surely had to join my architectural language.

Santa Monica: The Carpet with Frayed Edges

Comfort is surely a reasonable objective, yet recent generations have tended to sneer at it as any form of background for creativity. Rather to acknowledge the existence of some giant battleground out there where the only combat worth having is a struggle for the minds and hearts of the masses—or for certain influential sections of the masses. Yet finding a place in which you are extremely comfortable, but still consciously a visitor and thus an observer, can be highly creative. You have no obligation to the place, but neither do you have to take part in any local push-and-pull. You can drift around it, delighting (but quietly) in a mood reminiscent of nostalgia but not exactly looking-back. So I can have a wry but supportive smile at Santa Monica's smugness and its brilliant near-avoidance of dullness. Perhaps enjoying my English provincial's taste for the atmosphere of the *nuance*. Or the knowledge that some of the most exotic creativity of the late twentieth century lies hereabouts: from Frank Gehry's computerized antennae mapping out exotica for the shores of distant rivers, through the animation of dreams and cyborgs to the extension of the known universe via rocketry or digitalized sound. That this work is often conceived in versions of noddy houses or fairly nonchalant sheds creates its own piquancy. And all of this within a fairly ordinary American carpet. Thirty or so blocks deep and frayed at the edges.

So, too, are its constituent buildings frayed. The more recent fashionableness of Santa Monica has seen to it that the fraying is sometimes an applied aesthetic, but there is nothing as deliberate as the consistent high style in Art Nouveau Brussels or Berlin's Grunewald villas. Like the designer loafers, the crumpled T-shirt, the Marcuse compendium under the soda, or any local poolside banter: Southern Californian chic is unlike any other. Only the occasional talk of the Big One: the seismic conscience-symbol that must have had its parallels in ancient Athens, where similarly extremely lucky and intelligent citizens knew they were onto a good thing and feared its demise.

For my architecture, there might seem to be very little of substance that I can grab from the built form, its technology, or its ethics. But much to be taken from the conversations with architects there who (apart from Eric Moss in nearby Culver City) all seem to build elsewhere in overtly grubbier and busier cities, and then fly back to this ostensibly unbusy suburb. Much to be taken from a languid but cute observation of signals thrown out at the edges of the homestead, the condo, the corner lot, the strip mall, the reconstructed shed, the neat yuppie-tank. The city of Houston, which I will visit later, sends out some of the same signals but without the same relaxedness and only infrequently with the same range of mannerisms. By comparison, Santa Monica has just enough weather rather than climate

Typical scenery, Santa Monica.

and certainly a wider range of successful eccentrics enjoying it. So much can be taken from the accumulation of experiences of the Los Angeles conurbation. It has already been able to absorb everything from Arnold Schoenberg and Igor Stravinsky through to John Cage. Captivate F. Scott Fitzgerald and Chandler through to Umberto Eco. Provide for Josef Von Sternberg or John Huston through to Spielberg. But in architecture, perhaps the most brilliantly diverse list through Eames or Lautner to Gehry, Moss, Morphosis, Denari, and beyond.

Santa Monica is a living ghost city.

I only began to believe in creative ghosts while staying at Cranbrook, where I could feel the presence of old man Saarinen, young man Saarinen, Corbusier, Buckminster Fuller—the lot, passing through this imploded territory. So far Santa Monica is a bit looser than that, but to the sensitive nose it is already showing signs of something akin to the "séance" quality of Weimar, the Paris of Les Six, Black Mountain College, Taliesin, or the Vienna Secession.

It was in Westwood, a mile up the hill from Santa Monica, that I honed the English version of **Instant City** while Ron Herron, working nearby, located his version straightforwardly in West Los Angeles. There is a simultaneous memory of the English seaside and the fairground overlaid by day-to-day observation of the so-called Googie architecture (the most exotic example, "Ships" of Westwood, still existed well into the 1970s, down on the end of my street). At the same time Arata Isozaki from Tokyo and some of the Grazer Schule architects taught alongside me and fellow members of Archigram at UCLA. A rapid, sunny, escapist, eminently absorptive overlay of people and place. It was eleven years later that I came to teach at SCI-ARC during a critical phase of my work on **Arcadia**. The project has never had any other "mind's-eye" context than southeastern England . . . more explicitly, the Suffolk-Essex border, and its toughest street refers to somewhere between New York and Hamburg. Yet the looseness of conversations in Santa Monica is exactly paralleled by the considerable quantity of loose matter oozing out around the set pieces of Arcadia City. Already Santa Monica was shifting from being an American variant of Eastbourne—but on the West Coast—toward a conscious sophistication. Nowadays you only have to count the number of bookstores. So if one's architecture is unashamedly involved in stretching its vocabulary, the opening and reopening of the portmanteau to include successive discoveries is part of the game. These "discoveries" are more likely than not to be compilations of things glimpsed with things already known. Keeping the lid constantly open and especially so in relaxed circumstances, for a relaxed mood and a wry glance work very well together.

Santa Monica seen from the Getty Institute.

INSTANT CITY
(Peter Cook, 1968–69)
Drawn while in Los Angeles but applied to an English field. The "city" rides in like a circus and contains real or simulated city culture but stays only for a week.

Tokyo: The Hidden Villages

Tokyo is vast, and statistically, formally, politically, culturally it should be alarming. But it isn't. First of all, the "doughnut" condition (though hardly fair in a city with little public open space) is a great boon. Only on one day a year is the populace allowed to enter the central space of the doughnut: the Imperial Palace gardens. The rest of the time it exists as a secret lung and the first ring of centers: Ginza, Marunouchi, Jimbo-Cho, and Nagata-cho circle it. Immediately there is space, distance across which to orient or identify. And then the city really begins: those tough, sometimes winding, sometimes two- or even three-level main streets shoot up away from the doughnut and demarcate the localities. Yet, as in London or Paris, these streets *are* the life of the city. Tokyo's architecture has never been squeamish and has never been too rigidly proscribed by the type of planning rules that lead to even spread, even height, even tone, or even expression. The exercise of money, power, or aspiration wears its motives openly along these big streets. After a few days you can know the city quite well since there are always sufficient idiosyncrasies to be read along the way.

You can know it as a visitor with busy things to do among these overt, corporate blocks. But if you have friends living there, if you have time to wander, if you suddenly have any reason to poke around behind these big streets, another Tokyo is revealed—or, it must be, a thousand other Tokyos.

The address card will show a small map, the Chome will be revealed—but only cursorily. It can never be fully revealed since the grain seems to wrap and wrap and wrap: everything from a roof down to a milk carton seems to be knitted and tucked into each other. True, there are building envelopes and doorways. More articulate than these, however, are the ubiquitous drink machines that appear with something like the frequency that manholes have in London. For the locals there must be constant thirst and then a scampering away down into a mysterious crevice and into the tucks and folds.

Of course, the life inside has its laptops and deep-freezes, though characteristically tucked and folded into spaces rather less than in most Western cities. The enjoyment of life, the necessities for comfort, and the willingness to act out the folding and tucking: the essentially appliqué nature of Tokyo's hidden villages is perhaps more than an aesthetic matter. This is what you want to think as you spend your first evening playing with the

Typical back street, Tokyo.

Akasaki district, Tokyo.

paper screen, tracing the trajectory of the wiring system, indulging in the fifty qualities of light that seem to flow mysteriously between screened sun, filtered mist, or hinted shadow. The same niceties that accrue from a culture that has learned well how to mix and hide so many codes: protocol, implied protocol, veiled protocol, the overt private life, the private-private life, the secret private life. Food displays the same framework of symbolism, aesthetic and post-rationalization so that you may survive on a crowded, damp island. This is an obvious culture to be enjoyed, observed, and then transferred back into the hidden village: another clueing system into its perplexing grain.

You abandon the aesthetic issue as a motive. It is in fact a loose series of crusts that wraps the search for privacy. It is in fact a remnant of the more typical generic system of Japanese villages and towns that have never been high powered enough to acquire the big stuff along the main street. It is the actual Tokyo; the other is an incrustation. Alternatively, you can treat the two Tokyos as an interdependent system. But this too seems to miss the point. The old Soho in London, cut through by Regent Street, the old districts of Paris inserted by scalpel with Haussmann's boulevards: they seem to articulate themselves well enough, pulling the big stuff into themselves, exposing the odd tantalizing glimpse to the main street. Such push-and-pull is less common in Tokyo.

Or is it that one's seduction by the apparent mysteriousness of the "village" has been so great that one wants to keep the two cities apart? I travel selfishly. I ponder on what I might find useful. There is too fine a dividing line between peeking and appropriating. My visits to Tokyo coincided with a period in which I was trying to interlace the unlike with the unlike. The villages combined the incongruous with the nonchalant: the window with the tent, the air-con box with the decorated surface, the clipped-on with the woven-in, the garish with the elegant, the deep and mysterious with the bland and the frontal—my years of correction were being peeled away. What of all those European generic types: generic houses, generic streets, generic offices, generic doorways? The naughty seaside kid who had been scratching away, hoping that one day all cities could be like the world on top of the pier: had he not been waiting all this time to scamper around a Tokyo village?

Another thing before we leave. Why is it that so many of these hidden paradises are on small hills? Islands of clever muddle between estuaries of obviousness?

Typical "hinterland" area, Yushima district, Tokyo.

Edinburgh: Patches of Building against the Rock

As it hugs the great rock, Edinburgh Castle knits insidiously into its very substance. It is very lucky. Most buildings are of humbler background. For them, the space has to be found, haggled over, borrowed, cleared, pinned into, and the very authority of the built object itself is the product of issues of toleration, misunderstanding, and misuse. For the ancient Scots, sitting on the rock meant power, building into that rock with hewn pieces of rock meant the augmentation of that power. The recognizably operational or symbolic parts of the castle that came later fitted into the same system. So, unlike our cautious or self-conscious cottages, villas, or terraces, the castle at Edinburgh was able to develop itself from natural lump, natural chunk, and through to special hunk with the greatest of ease. It was the nearest thing in former times to the current use of the "morph" instruction to the computer.

Every time I look at that castle I am envious of its homogeneity as well as its morphological spread. No wonder the old town of Edinburgh could only creep gingerly up toward it and the new town of Edinburgh sits at a rather polite distance, on the other side of the gardens. In a number of projects I have tried to suggest that such a metamorphosis is possible—through time, of course, as a way of throwing the onus onto circumstance, change of circumstance, the natural need for adaptation. In the **city hall for Arcadia**, I attempt to make a crystalline Edinburgh Castle: working the rock in reverse. Start with the formal, the gestural part: the tower. Then establish the solid and regular body: the secretariat. Then suggest that certain suborganizations would be allowed to infiltrate; I represent them as imperfections or dissections of the solid . . . and, in the manner of "one thing leads to another" I will the progressive disintegration of both organization and form until we are left with a form of "heap" that can merge with the mounded park. In other parts of Arcadia and in later projects, I return to this dilemma. Is it only possible to melt or disintegrate a piece of architecture if the status of that which is to be melted is assured? Can you start somewhere in the middle and just harden or soften the proposition?

Certainly this is a far cry from the Tokyo village, where any search for the consistent loses you the thread. Yet in my warped, alchemic mind, the idea of variation without composition is worth pursuit. Both from the hard end and the soft.

Edinburgh Castle nestles into the rock.

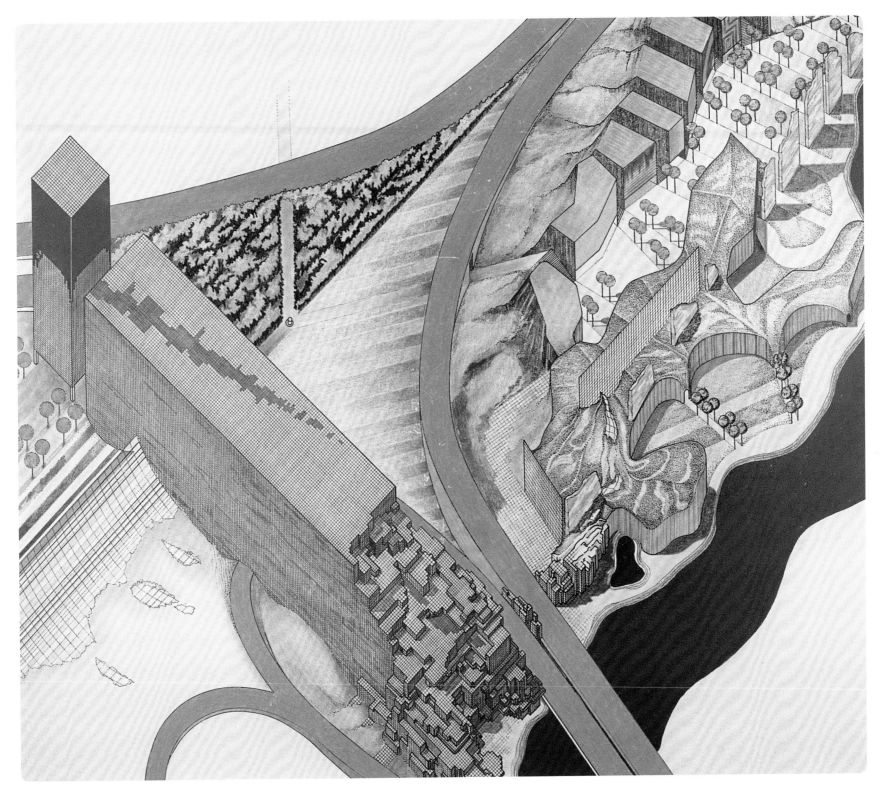

ARCADIA CITY: THE CITY HALL
(Peter Cook, 1978)
The "official" building starts heroically, then progressively fragments and melts completely into the structure of wayward sheds and gardens.

Stockholm: Continuing the City across Water and Time

In the search for the casual city, the frayed suburb, the impenetrable village, the contiguous mass, there is, in each case, an implicit lack of interruption. One place will lead to another. The city grain is dependent upon its will to coagulate. Yet one of the most tantalizing of all cities appears to defy that maxim, for Stockholm exists quite coherently despite the dramatic fractures that are made by the sea. Its architecture, too, is a mixture of the solid and the coy—that characteristic of Scandinavian late Classicism that became absorbed into its Modernism. So was Layer City a wish to bring Stockholm to the Oslo Fjord? Or is another clue my train of thought that searches for an analogy between the islands of village behind the big streets of Tokyo and the islands that make up the total city of Stockholm? More likely it is that heavily instilled need for reference that all persuasions of architectural teaching seem to resort to. Developed as a discipline, a rationale, a procedure. Create the primary matrix, the key lines of reference. The cuts of demarcation. *Then* we can play.

Stockholm intrigues because it is made up of so many incidents and its waterside is rarely overheroic; nor is it thrown away. Its avenues are there, but controlled. Yet it is not flimsy in its picturesqueness. It seems to offer the ideal balance of forces, yet its architectural alchemy is fairly predictable. The timing of the incidents, too, is evenly spread, for Stockholm does not seem to have suffered too much drama in the last three hundred years. The referencing marks are therefore equally calm and usefully wayward: build where there's land and don't where there's water.

If all cities were as simple they might all be as beautiful.

In Stockholm, the islands hardly seem to inhibit the presence of an elegant and highly iconic city. Cohesion successfully jumps the water.

Landing quays, Stockholm.

London: Where You Need Not Ever Know

The hardest to know, even after forty years of more or less continuous presence there. But perhaps that is its trick. Like the English friendship, it constantly seems to hold off any declaration of interest. There are enough circumstantial and muddled cities in the world for us to avoid the obviousness of contrasting its organization with that of Paris, Washington, or Barcelona. There are other cities, too, in which the structure of the old villages creates a physiognomy of strange focal points: those of Bucharest are more frequent and more mysterious, those of Vienna more insidiously incorporated into an apparently hierarchical logic. In London there seems to be a separate rule for each. The church on the hill as focus . . . no. The church by the little river . . . no. The village clinging to the edge of the big field . . . no. The village lining the highway . . . no. The village still there, somewhere behind the highways. The cut village. The lost river. The smothered market. The drained marsh.

To compound any further stacking up of the evidence in nice, neat categories, there are the delights of English eccentricity. You need look no further than John Vanbrugh or John Soane to realize that the key English Classicists were too bored and far too inventive to stick to the rules. You need look no further than to examine the way in which its river is bridged, ignored, celebrated, and generally treated like an old sock and then—very, very recently—rediscovered for all the best or worst picturesque reasons.

Just as you get a taste for its eccentric delights you may be plummeted into the necessity of living in one of its vast areas of developer-suburbs. Infinitely more tedious than those of Brooklyn or Brussels, especially those English suburbs built between 1870 and 1910. The Gothic tweaks, repeated a thousand times, only serve to remind us of the formulaic nature of the houses themselves. Eventually, of course, there will be a break in the system: an encounter with a winding highway, a patch of eccentricities, then more eccentricities and, for a mile or so, we can indulge in the real. Let's say the *preferred* London of secret delights.

The inner suburbs of London—large gardens and semidetached housing (circa 1905).

The outer suburbs, London. The same tradition continues.

Look over a simple, deadpan wall. My God! Another building of quite a different kind from the rest: knitted in, hanging out, almost (but not quite) screening us from yet another hidden building of yet another kind. Don't think that you've twigged the system, for across the street contrary signals will be transmitted. A quite different urban grain, another incident. The picturesque flanked by the bland. And vegetation, always plenty of vegetation—even in some of those gray suburbs. Rarely as "sweet" or as clean as Oslo. Never as fine-grained as Tokyo. Hardly as relaxed as Santa Monica, yet there are even some echoes of these to be found.

There is the garden wall, as well as the inner and outer reaches of the garden to be considered as territories. So many London buildings hang out at the back, in a variety of ramshackle increments. And then there is the garden proper. If it is deep, there may be another zone available for even more ramshackle buildings or sheds of various kinds. These rarely reach the status of the German *hofhaus* but in rare cases they are, surreptitiously, working buildings. The result is a continuity of the building/planting ambiguity: not a legitimate form or system but undoubtedly powerful as an inspiration, implying "softness" and encouraging a feeling of continuity less hard or dramatic as *bricolage,* a concept that has reluctantly been permitted a place in European architectural thinking. This drifting, tacky, half-planted, charming London thing lacks the collagist's built-unbuilt definition, and because of this it reiterates its influence on me. I have to work hard not to be seduced into its tackiness. I have to work hard to reinvent it as the legitimate expression of organisms that (of course) have a procedure or even a consistency. Yet in every project from **Sponge** and **Arcadia** in the 1980s through to **Super-Houston** twenty years later, these insidious growths of London-backs are to be found lurking among the contrivance of the constructed and the vegetated knitwear. They have only occasionally had a London location, yet it is in that city that most of the conversations have been held. And I must admit there has always been a tree or two outside the window.

Taken at its lowest level, London always has a trick or two to be observed—so long as it isn't a strictly *architectural* trick.

TAIL

Architects : Peter Cook and Yael Reisner 1996...ongoing

The infiltration of one's own (early 1900's) apartment in South Hampstead by a modelled skin starts to ricochet out into the garden. So far without 'claws', the skin is easily able to wander around desired pockets within and then wander on outside so as to create an 'evening-suncatcher'. Tweaking the edge of the garden from time to time and ending as a prototype summerhouse. The tail will continue to develop : not necessarily as any more skin, but with more devices sneaking out from it.

In this way, the 1930s fascination with 'garden-infiltrating-house' is reversed : a fragmented alternative to the white courtyard of the Mediterranean is offered by something that - along with its Modernism - even has the occasional memory of vistas and gazebos, English narrativism and trailing echoes.

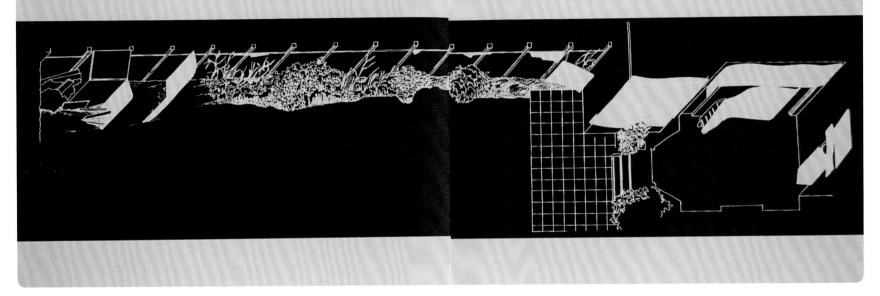

"TAIL" PROJECT
(Peter Cook and Yael Reisner, ongoing)
An internal "flowing skin" ricochets out into the garden, depositing elements of itself: white against thick vegetation.

2

THE CITY OF ATMOSPHERES

Berlin

With a turbulent history that seems to have reached a crescendo during the period of my youth, Berlin presented to such a detached Englishman that weird combination of folly and grandeur, mystery and decay, as well as a series of mythologies: Isherwood's Berlin, Hitler's Berlin, Scharoun's Berlin, Wenders's Berlin. Or the dispossessed and divided town of immense energy that I actually discovered in the early 1970s. The first sight of Ludwig Leo's Umlauftank—the blue box on green legs sitting above the exotic pink pipe—was a revelation on three counts. First, it rekindled my enthusiasm for high-powered constructive form just at the moment when my own work had ebbed away from such things and toward a "soft" and discrete architecture (it was the period of **Addhox**, the **Hedgerow Village,** and the **Lump** project). Second, this building was the nearest thing to Iakov Tchernikov's illustrations in his 101 Fantasies book—a cult reference for me at the AA school in 1960—but realized as uncompromisingly (and essentially colored) as those far-away images of a future architecture. It was undoubtedly real—sitting there, gurgling away in a corner of the canal near the Technische Hochschule. Third, it was never mentioned abroad: somehow it lay outside the direct, explainable story of Modern German architecture. So it tempted me from then on to make any number of myths about the potential of Berlin as a hiding place, in the way of London, perhaps.

Beyond this, the legitimacy of Berlin as an architectural powerhouse over the whole of the twentieth century just seemed to confirm itself over and over again. Mendelsohn's Universum Cinema (soon to be converted into a theater) still seemed fresh in that way of being a *living diagram*; the social housing of the 1920s and 1930s still seemed fresh and eminently livable. Even the Hansaviertel of the 1950s (though by then at a low point in its reputation) did not disappoint me; rather, it confirmed my book-learned admiration for Niemeyer, Aalto, and the rest. And the Philharmonie? Again, like the Umlauftank, it confirmed my dreams that there could be such a thing as "direct" architecture. By this, I suppose I mean an architecture of deliberate configuration that comes out of its own spirit and trajectory. Or do I mean an architecture that avoids recognizing whole series of acknowledgments to culture, meaning, history, statement, context, or the niceties of inherited tectonic procedures? An attitude that was inherently unfashionable for all those reasons at any time in the last thirty years.

**BERLIN, BREITSCHEIDPLATZ PROJECT,
AXONOMETRIC**
(Peter Cook, 1994)
Picking up the energy of the corners,
then wrapping and reflecting.

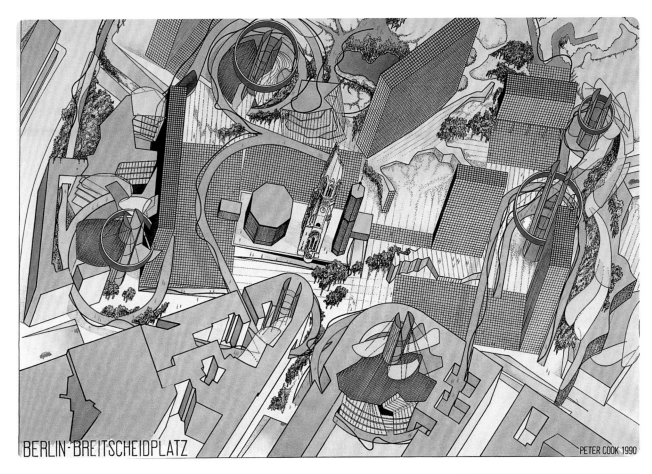

**BERLIN, BREITSCHEIDPLATZ PROJECT,
ELEVATION**
(Peter Cook, 1994)

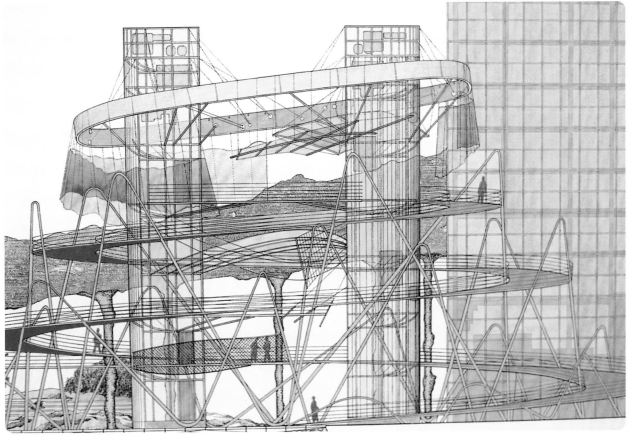

Umlauftank (hydraulics testing station), Berlin.
(Ludwig Leo, 1965)

Breitscheidplatz area, Berlin. The occasional 1950s gem nestles under an otherwise undistinguished office block.

Schaubrunne, Berlin.
(Eric Mendelsohn, 1929)
Cinema readapted as a "black box" auditorium.

Breitscheidplatz, Berlin. The war-damaged Kaiserkapelle reinstated by Egon Eiermann in the 1950s.

Even without the wall, Berlin retains the ability to hide and at the same time to shout out the presence of an event. The atmosphere of the city moves rapidly from elation to depression, from joy to cowering grimness. Some of this was, I believe, quite contrived, related not to the turbulence of history but more to the Prussian recognition of achievement and role play. If Kreuzberg and Friedrichshain were essentially "servant" areas to the central city, their attractions were few. If Charlottenburg or Steglitz were permitted more airs and graces (but still a limit on their escape from duty), then must the coy escapism of Zehlendorf or Gatow also be part of a deliberate plan? London sustains some of the same cynical class-consciousness in the contrast between Hampstead and Bethnal Green or between Campden Hill and Shoreditch. In long, long streets; hard, hard blocks; deep, deep courtyards. London would break down some part of its shell. Berlin was only forced to do so by the effects of shelling and bombing. Berlin had been a get-rich-quick working city as well as a capital. It had built up a toughness that even Hamburg's docklands could not emulate. In those parts of the year when there is no barrier to the wind between the long, long streets and the Urals, a cozy doorway becomes a triumph of survival. The hallway within a further celebration; even the courtyard of a sweatshop making cheap shirts becomes a cosseted microclimate. Thus, Berlin played with its millions of exploiters and exploited, arriving mostly from the East.

By the time that I could pick up on any of this, the craters and fissures that exposed this tyranny had been tinkered with and, in many cases, refilled. Mostly with a bland but chunky concrete Modernism and some jolly colored panels. Encouraged in the early 1990s to look at the **Breitscheidplatz** as a project, I realized how far I had been seduced by the convenience of an easy architecture sitting among brooding remnants. I was most fascinated by this place as a focus for aimless wandering—strolling in the evening, coming from the zoo with the kids, general shopping and looking—or a place for almost anybody to hang out. Now that there is no barrier, Berliners from the East also seem to like to hang out there. Dramatic focus? Of course there is: with the Kaiserkapelle standing as a scarred ruin filled up by Egon Eiermann's swathes of concrete-held window points: a counterpoint that still works theatrically and iconographically, even for a generation that wonders what it was all about.

Around, but at a distance, lie a variety of slablike buildings created with logic but little magic, very reasonable and unmemorable. It is easy to say that they hardly rise to the occasion of their moment of history, that they could just as easily fit the center of Mannheim or Kiel as that of this very special metropolis. Ironically though, Kantstrasse, Budapeststrasse, Tauentzienstrasse—not to speak of the unforgettable Kurfurstendamm—all radiate from this place and all, within a few blocks, engage with the typically powerful pieces of pomposity or action that remind us that we are in this wicked city.

So the Breitscheid blocks needed a reaction: mine was to cloak all these slabs in a common grid and pull that same grid down onto the ground: a permanent drifting cloak or "shadow" of equal size to the slab. Now they would speak in a chorus of patches. As a counterpoint, I used the symbolic geometry that reminds me most of the kind of drifting that I might do on a slow city walk: a meander, a soft gyration. Picking up on the two big rounded corners on the south side of the platz, probably a remainder of the 1910s or 1920s, I started a series of gyrating paths that wandered round and up, drifted across, wend their way down, and occasionally cut into the fabric, generally enjoying themselves and spawning a deliberately untidy architectural sponge from time to time. In its curious way a preservationist scheme—if bulk and form are to be the criterion—but iconoclastic if figure and surface mean more.

A few blocks away, Christine Hawley and I were building a piece of housing on another West Berlin platz. I had made a film with Hessischer Rundfunk on the Internationale Bau-Ausstellung (the IBA), which was a response to the Hansa Viertel of the 1980s generation. Where Hansa offered open grass between idiosyncratic islands of building, IBA pledged itself to the reconstitution of the Berlin blocks. In my film I had been somewhat critical of the results thus far, managing to incorporate simultaneous homage to Leo's tank, or eavesdropping with camera and microphone upon the creative cynicism of James Stirling in his Hampstead House and Raimund Abraham in his New York loft, or dwelling for ten minutes on the creative eccentricity of Hinrich Baller, who simultaneously made his own harpsichords and his own Baroque housing. Implying that most of the rest were playing out some pretty thoughtless Postmodernism that would soon look tired, especially when locked into a twenty-one-meter-high solid block. So someone in the organization must then have thought, OK, if you think you're so smart, how about having a try yourself?

At the **Lutzowplatz**, Christine and I circled around the issue. We started from basic principles of "heap-up." We distorted the roofline. We deflected and drifted the lines of force. But most of all we adopted that essentially English habit of starting on the inside and letting it all (conceptually) hang out. Continually walking around the apartments, inventing stories of "joke" families—with silly goings-on to test out the corners, the nooks, the balconies, and most of all, the sight lines.

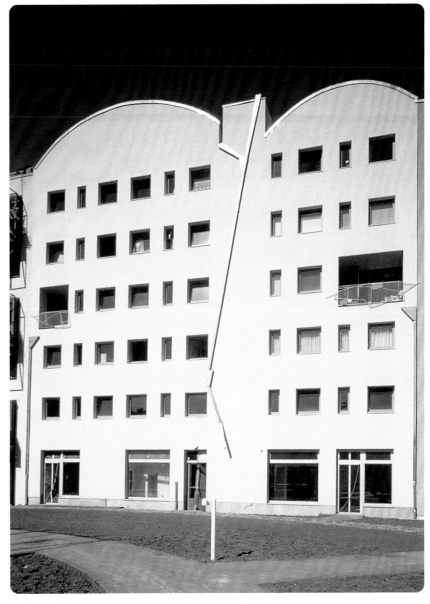

WEST SIDE OF LUTZOWPLATZ HOUSING, BERLIN
(Waltraud Krase)
The extrovert and active side faces the Lutzowplatz gardens
and, beyond them, the Tiergarten.

EAST SIDE OF LUTZOWPLATZ HOUSING, BERLIN
(Waltraud Krase)
Bedrooms and bathrooms on the quiet courtyard side create a
(nearly) rationalist facade.

In many respects, our little patch was ideal. The yard at the back was to the east. The platz (more of a small park, with trees and bushes) at the front was to the west, with long views into the Tiergarten. We might claim that the building designed itself. We evolved a larger range of apartments than might seem circumspect: seven types in fourteen units, "barn" on the top, a "railway station" alongside.

Small-scale tricks to kick up the implicit "boxiness" of late-twentieth-century housing: with a couple of steps up to the eating/cooking area and a subsequent uplift of the ceilings above and below. Small chinks of view as you skip through to the bathroom in the middle of the night. More views as you prepare the salad. Internal "towers," to give a hierarchy to the inevitable boxiness of kitchen fittings. And a modest exercise in layering on the west side.

You must remember that the **Shadow House**, the **Layer City**, and the **Sponge** were excursions into the idea of layering surfaces and even layering functioning parts: one in front of the other. One slithering past the other. Often irregularly, often with soft definition of "edge" or "patch." Some hint of this is contained in the west elevation, where drifting parts and layers of perforated metal run past the glass.

In each apartment, there is some sense of being in a pavilion, of directly enjoying the sylvan scene of small park in the foreground, large park in the distance, and hint of grandeur coming from the obelisk of the Grosser Stern in the middle of the Tiergarten.

The Piquant Memory

As a child living in Ipswich, I easily absorbed the mix of market town, port, and industry with well-preserved historical set pieces. Ancient houses, gates, churches, and streets—the predominantly nineteenth-century mix of a pleasant industrial town. Yet one image was to haunt me for years (and, with delight, I recently found that it still exists, just as I had remembered it). On a busy street, a frequently open door reveals a dark corridor at the end of which one can just see green, smoky light. An impressionable memory of seeing the ballet *The Green Table* at the age of six added to the impact, for it was a billiard hall.

There is nothing too sinister about billiards or about that particular street in Ipswich, and indeed, I was not actually scared, but edgily intrigued. In the same way that I was in 1958 when, unexpectedly, I came upon a Dada exhibition in Düsseldorf on my first-ever day in Germany. It is the same feeling that I get when contemplating photographs of the café in Strasbourg by Van Doesburg—a piquancy that comes from unexpected juxtaposition, not just stimulated by form but also by oddness perhaps.

This is a very difficult ingredient to build into a design. Sure, you can posit a series of shapes or deliberate challenges to the local culture (which I shall discuss in Chapter 4), but this quality of localized strangeness has something to do with contrast, yet the contrast must not be announced too soon. It has much to do with expectancy and the homogeneity of cities; certainly the search for such a quality is worth pursuing, though it only seems to occur in the oddest circumstances.

The Wry Search

It is even worth the discomfort of the full heat of the summer to wander around the streets of the 1920s and 1930s city of Tel Aviv and, as it cools, to wander more deviously and watch the place in operation. That the best collection of "white" Modernism exists there is well known. But the books and photographs concentrate on villas, apartments, perhaps the odd cinema: on set pieces, or advanced configurations of boulevard, street, vegetated enclave. They are layered into this city of enterprise, which is inhabited by individuals who put more energy and determination into selling an idea, some insurance, or a pair of trainers than anyone else in the world. As it was a city of rapid growth and continues as a city of opportunism, the turnover of use, misuse, and reuse is sharp. The architectural clarity of the 1930s buildings serves to highlight the paradoxical quality and the detail of *life* in a way that the softer forms, the grayer light, and the more ambiguous weather of Northern Europe tends to hide. The most telling details on the street are the small display boxes and the boulevard kiosks. Such boxes can be found on the Kurfurstendamm in Berlin, meticulous in their upkeep and the discrimination with which the most enticing merchandise directs you a few meters across the sidewalk to an equally enticing shop. Not quite so on Ben Jehudah Street in Tel Aviv. The detailing is identical, but the surfaces are unkempt, the merchandise either not there at all or lost in time, consisting of strange pamphlets, out-of-date alarm clocks, or dead flies. Yet the cars swishing disinterestedly past are the same models as in Berlin and of equally recent vintage.

On an opposite corner, a two-meter sliver of space might be occupied by an enterprising seller of old paperback books—in a variety of languages—doing brisk trade. In my favorite "street of enterprise" two dozen or more shops sell watches, bracelets, cheap cameras, and maybe fountain pens. Few have customers. The Tel-Avivian kiosk, on the other hand, is busy, well painted, and surrounded by a "clubby" clientele; it may well sport a chirpy mural and even a second enterprise grafted onto the rear. By contrast, the Berlin

Kiosk on Ben Gurion Avenue, Tel Aviv.

Shoe repair cabin,
Allenby Street, Tel Aviv.

Display case on Ben
Yahudah Street, Tel Aviv.

Kiosk on Dizengoff Street, Tel Aviv.

Typical street from the 1930s city, Tel Aviv.

version tends to be more tired, more resigned to selling second-class liquor and dodgy biscuits, with the incumbent resigned to the situation.

The boulevards and street cafés give a clue to the desire of the original inhabitants of Tel Aviv to continue the civilized ways of Berlin or Vienna. The architecture was of the newest kind, and the boxes, kiosks, and shops were designed to respond. Yet in Tel Aviv, as elsewhere, today's bourgeoisie has chosen to drive to a mall, park in comfort, and shop or gossip in surroundings similar to those of Cincinnati or Lille: in air-conditioned comfort. The particularities of corners, alleys, street edges, passages, doorways, backsides, and the possible choreography that results from topography, upsides, downsides, right or wrong sides are decreasingly attractive to investors. They may be remembered or confined to poorer areas of big cities. Yet a study of their effect upon behavior has tremendous potential. It would involve the behavior of the built carcass, as well as that of the users, and of every category of go-between device: awnings, windows, machinery, outriders, advertising, places to hover, places to rush, places to escape. In making and drawing proposals for a design, there is a danger that one can only get involved by introducing more and more detail. There is an annoyance with this, coming partially from the inheritance of Modernism and equally from the experience of commercial design. In the end, one is searching for a subtle method of hierarchical involvement. Observing the day-to-day event and making marks that might imply choreography—or at least, create a template for choreographic acts.

Allenby Street, the first high street of 1920s Tel Aviv, is a portent of what may happen to Oxford Street, Fifth Avenue, or the Kurfurstendamm in the future: it has the greatest density of ambiguous trading activity taking place in the greatest variety of misused space that I know of. Yet because of this I meander along it sensing the same edgy piquancy that adds quality to practical activity.

The European Café

European architects are the best guide to eating and drinking of any social group. Straight indulgence or value for money mix together with the issue of ambience, and the chosen venues are often in sharp contrast to the mannerisms of their own architecture. Intriguing patterns do emerge, despite all this. First, the issue of statement to the street. A café or restaurant is not a shop: it may even wish to appear off-putting so that the clientele will be left alone by tourists and provincials, though this has not been the fate of the Café Hawelka in Vienna, certainly the preferred haunt of the 1960s and 1970s experimenters but now abandoned by them and left to tourists and provincials. The exterior is shabby and shrouded, the interior tacky, but it retains its mythology. That the special table used by Hans Hollein and Walter Pichler in their formative days was in a hidden corner facing the view and odor of the men's room questions our well-brought-up attitudes concerning hierarchy of space!

At the Theatercafeen in Oslo, a far more overt and developed sense of theater exists. Still subdued from the street (all one sees is a row of modest arched windows as they move around a corner), you enter a lobby and then turn into the fin-de-siècle restaurant along a narrow "arm" (this is the area used by journalists). Bursting into the double-height space, you discover that there are areas for businesspeople, theater people, architects, and those engaged in discreet tête-à-têtes. And the tourists? They are shoved deep into the far arm, ranged in front of a giant mirror. The maintenance of an orchestra that always plays *slightly* out of tune is a further offering. How can we design such a combination of features? Can we anticipate the escape of the journalists from the sound of the orchestra while simultaneously vetting everyone who comes in for a story? Can we insist on an undercroft beneath any balcony where the eccentricity of the musicians is a calculated decoy from the private world beneath?

The bar and restaurant areas of the Hotel Avion in Brno are even more intriguingly carved out, with amazing slots of space, changing in profile, dimension (and surely *intention*) as they move up the building. Even in a seedy state and in the daytime—as they were when I went there in the 1980s with my students—it held a sense of intrigue, with a piquant flavor similar to the Ipswich doorway. One could only speculate upon its role in the scenarios of intellectuals and their hangers-on in Brno society for over seventy years. Yet the denial of full ambience puts a pressure on our ways of remembering, recording, or predicting. It puts tremendous pressure on the act of drawing, for drawing can simultaneously track a

Café Hawelka in the inner city: artists (formerly), tourists (now).

Café Sperl, Vienna: conscious fin de siècle in a trendy neighborhood.

Café Wien, Vienna: market traders and intellectuals.

Reiss Bar, Vienna: Coop Himmelblau (in an early built work) displays its Viennese credentials.

Theatercaffeen, Oslo.

Restaurant area, Hotel Avion, Brno.

Lobby, Hotel Royal, Madrid.

wide variety of issues: position, density, hierarchy, and under certain circumstances, atmosphere. Drawing can also create optimistic lies. We increasingly use photographs and Photoshop collage in the same way, but how can we predict "chatter" or "exclusiveness" or any implicit intentions of a room except by way of surmise?

In the Britannia Hotel in Trondheim, Norway, a dining room in an approximation of Moorish style contains tall palm trees. The room is entered from the street after passing through several layers of corridor. For one thousand kilometers in any direction there is no room as elegant. The nearest palms are probably even farther away. It is the creation of a myth with real ingredients. From now on, virtual-reality techniques will add to the possibility of such escapist scenes. For the observant connoisseur there may be Nordic giveaways in the mannerism of such a room. For the arch connoisseur these giveaways will add to the ambience, giving it a quality far more intriguing than straight Moorish spaces for real Moors.

The other message that the characteristic street café can give is a simple offering of three or four related spaces. Our reaction to them will define *us* as interpreters of the building—and we will have to go along with its implications. Sitting under the canopy of Les Deux Magots in Paris, we display our presence. Sitting far forward in the interior, we are still able to observe the activities on the street—and to be recognized by the observant. A location deep within may be a statement about discretion or privacy. And a seat on the upper floor? Either a heroic move or an admission of total failure. How many of us, when shuffled into the part of the café that we had *not* desired, have post-rationalized and thought of all the reasons why it's all right anyway? Certain designers believe (for social, political, or moral reasons) that all parts of the room are equal and even shy away from the scenography of such an analysis. For me, they are escaping from one of the key issues of place: as experience and as potential experience. The Hotel Avion explores this exhaustively; Les Deux Magots presents a layered stage. Neither is abstract. Neither is innocent.

In Glasgow there is a circular bar. You can just about make your way around the rim on a crowded night. Its clientele is varied: business suits mingle with artists who mingle with jocks. Only the entrance door at the corner implies some process of finding a suitable spot around the rim. Any coterie that forms is constantly blown open by the progress of a circulating interloper. Analytically it is either a brilliant or disastrous diagram. Brilliant if you enjoy Glaswegian humor and you are not shy. Disastrous if you believe in territory and position. A diagram that would be unthinkable in either Madrid or Cheltenham.

Round the Corner and Further Through

American cities are on grids, English cities are meandering, many European cities establish large swathes of a grid system, which is then broken by preexisting patterns of villages or fortifications. With deliberate misinterpretation of the system, a person can pick up on changes of atmosphere that do not exactly echo changes of fabric. Similarly, you can chose to recognize special icons, suddenly discovering them in a place you thought that you really knew. Stepping across a familiar street in Oslo, I turned to look for traffic and realized that the cathedral foreclosed the skyline in one direction and the steeple of a church at the other. But at the end of the road facing me was a Dragon-style point on the top of a building. So I turned round, just to check. Yes! There was a fourth spire, picking up the end of *that* axis. What to do? Was I the only person to recognize the special nature of this very spot, its magic, its simultaneous tension and reassurance?

It actually served to remind me of all the variety, history, and experience of the territories between: the change of atmosphere as you descended from these markers. The bourgeois Oslo drifting around the spires, the maritime city beyond the Dragon, the old roots around the cathedral.

I sited my four **Oslo Lantern Towers** on St. Olavsgate, the same street from which I had picked up the four points. I quoted the lantern at a variety of scales. First, at the scale of the large lanterns that were common in Oslo and Stockholm from the 1910s to the 1930s, occurring just above shop fascia level so that in the long evenings the street can be bright and articulated. The character of these lanterns is formally strong and original to the architecture of the particular building on which they sit. Some are more than a meter high.

At the next scale up, I drew an analogy between such lanterns and the tradition of the bay window. The scale moves up to three meters. These window-lanterns then move up to the scale of an expressed room: bursting out of the wall at the scale of four or six meters. Then, as one climbs up the tower, the whole apartment itself may be as a lantern; the scale is twelve meters or more. Finally, the whole top of the tower becomes a giant lantern.

Four lantern towers of equal height, seen at best by night. In the daytime, they have the grayed tones of Norwegian Funkis colors. They create an atmosphere of downtown at the scale of the skyline and encourage the intervention of pockets, alleys, crevices, and curious sight lines to collect around their lower girths.

OSLO TOWERS, DAYTIME
(Peter Cook, 1984)
The towers adopt the Norwegian Funkis coloration and provide a marker for the downtown area.

OSLO TOWERS, NIGHTTIME
At night, the towers offer a range of lantern conditions in various scales up to that of the tower itself: a giant lantern.

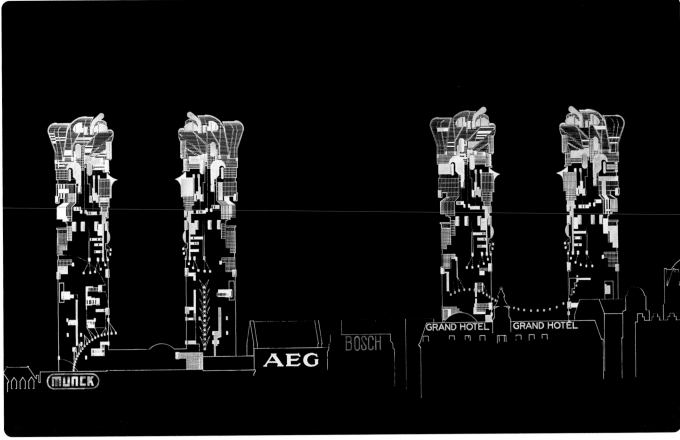

Sniffing Out a City

Walking through towns is my favorite pastime. Sniffing the scenery. Guessing the history. Playing games with recognition. "Obviously a shadow of its former self." . . . "*Something* is about to happen here." . . . "*That* building is totally out of place. What could have been the story?" One "collects" sinister streets, revealing corners, opaque facades, new territories, doorway vistas, glimpsed courtyards, quiet patches. As with the Tokyo villages, my supposition that the quiet areas are the greater clue to the psychology of a place may in fact be a form of Romanticism. Some cities even seem to be swathes of forgotten town, awaiting the rhetoric of the others. If Amsterdam is sweet display and Rotterdam tough action, what of The Hague? I like to think that its intriguing nothingness hides a special spirit. Dutch friends try to convince me that this is a myth.

The physiognomy of Haifa suggests an almost ideal background for a special atmosphere: a city on the side of a mountain, with small ravines that complicate the formula. Flora and fauna that give it a gentler surface: more Basel than Tel Aviv. It has a vivid port area and miles of honky-tonk stretching along the coast. Brilliant 1930s Modernism. But the most observant Israelis reassure you that it is a dead city: "Everyone is in bed by nine." The architect in me wants to will it otherwise. My attachment is to the idea of a city of three or four strata, my observation is of creeping seediness as you go down the mountain, of bourgeois assiduousness as you go up. Of mixy, mixy society among it all. But I am told that I read *too much* into it. Thus we either choose to ignore social experience and make special claims, or, more usefully perhaps, we "save" the abstraction of the model. We keep the idea of the potential of such a place and unconsciously requote it as *form* in our own projects.

One searches for vitality and sees it in the 11th arondissement of Paris with its topography and physical mix and bare-bones living. Immediately obvious is its "authenticity," its avoidance of the smugness or the contrived heroics of the touristy city. Perhaps, again, it is a Romantic yearning for the medieval, or at any rate, for nineteenth-century muddle?

Somehow, a hairline has to be drawn between the value of atmosphere and the trap of the picturesque, between the dynamic of atmosphere and the attraction of the Other. Shift of emphasis, however, is a stronger force to grapple with. Cities have power because the shifts are of many—and constantly varying—scales. The grain may last for a mile, interference for half a block, the eccentric elements on a 3:6:11:5:99 interval. The hidden pocket not in a typical position but near the edge. The real city yet farther round the corner and farther through.

Maybe such things can never be designed. But if only they could?

Haifa, the "inclined" city.

Preparing the Stage

Graz, the Baroque city.

The **Arcadia City** set up a series of six enclaves: the marshland for the dreamers; the ordered grid for the regular folk; the lofts area for the tough and active; another high-powered but more style-conscious pocket for conscious hedonists; a peninsula for the retired bourgeoisie to retreat to; and a zone with many trees and walls in which the suburban dream (with a touch of Oxford quadrangle mixed in) could be enjoyed. The mannerism of the apartments, their plan form, and certainly that of the ground between was all coerced toward the illustration of these six scenarios. In contrast, the **Super-Houston** city, designed twenty years later, appears to offer only two territories: the streets with houses under the trees and the long, congealed liner. Yet my attitudes toward social scenarios have become, if anything, more creatively cynical and more experienced. What may be changed—apart from all the shifts in architectural mannerism—is the *grain*. The grain of examination and the grain of form.

In the design for the **Museum of Antiquities** at Bad Deutsches Altenberg (more fully described in Chapter 7), Christine Hawley and I were all too aware of building on top of two thousand years of history while enjoying the now placid, vegetated hillside by the Danube. We were aware of making some small buildings as a series of instruments: clad in steel and geometrically linked to each other. Recognition, instead of being discovered (as in the Oslo street corner), is now the conscious generator. Since we were aware of the presence of the Roman remains lying somewhere *within*, the site of new architecture became a signaling system across space and time as much as a formal museum. The deliberate lightness and fragmentary nature of the components sheltering the relics surely derives more from those display boxes on the Berlin or Tel Avivian streets than from the tradition of the *significant Institution*. Perhaps the nonchalant device emitting veiled signals has its own, even longer history. Were it to be built, this assemblage would be an attempt to summarize several simultaneous issues of nostalgia, atmosphere, and reference—in one set of moves.

In a small square in Graz, the first **Kunsthaus** project that Colin Fournier and I designed (we called it **The Tongue**) would have sprung from the surface as a discrete (though oddly shaped) sliver of building that curls out of sight and climbs insidiously along the edge of the steep cliff on top of which stands the castle of Graz. The normalcy of the adjoining buildings and the fairy-tale character of the cliff backdrop already create an odd atmosphere. Add to this The Tongue. Add to that the light-bubbles bursting out of it. Add to that the uncompromisingly clear and new atmosphere of the gallery within and you have the beginnings of a formula for the creation of a series of totally contrasting elements that need each other, challenge each other, and set up the architectural equivalent of an odd taste in the mouth.

The task is the creation as well as the observation of a city of atmospheres.

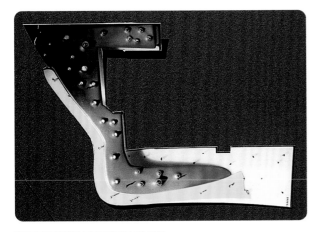

THE TONGUE PROJECT, GRAZ
(Peter Cook and Colin Fournier, 1998, model by David Ardill)

3

THE CITY OF PATHS, LAYERS, AND ROOMS

West Wycombe, the English prepared landscape.

Direction and Regulation

A fundamental conflict exists between the English attitude toward "going somewhere" and that of other cultures. The English subscribe to such notions as "to go is better than to arrive," or the instinctive feeling that if a destination is directly in front of one and the route to it is obvious, the story is over and the arrival almost certain to be a disappointment. Any number of associations can be brought to bear on this issue: the tendency for the English novel to be a series of meanderings toward a final situation that may be meaningful but not conclusive; the delight—in literature, drama, and aesthetics—for the fascinating aside, byway, counterplot, or glimpse; the tendency of the weather and the light to provide rapid changes of brightness and nuance (not the long weeks of gray of the real north, nor the long weeks of sun).

In England, eighteenth-century landscape gardeners drew on these tendencies and interpreted them, bringing them to the status of a high art. The progression through a piece of controlled countryside was a series of staged meanderings: the curve away from the obvious forward direction; the dramatically opened vista; the decoy lake, copse, or folly; the foreclosure of space followed by a sudden turn in direction; and many more. Where "plot" begins and "scenography" ends is a subtle and evolutionary process.

For me, the language of placing and arriving is still often primitive and seems if anything to have become more so of late, since the contemporary tendency toward optimization in all things, along with the power of accountant-pressure in most fields of operation, urges us to put things in an obvious place and make the route toward them equally obvious. Such a new primitiveness evokes a lack of guile. Yet in England we psychologically thrive upon a steady accumulation of bits and pieces that call themselves villages, lanes, hedges, pathways, woods, and an overlay of relics of all kinds that seem to diffuse the exposure of the objective. We let history protect us from directness, and even parody this casual accumulation with a recherché aesthetic that *pretends* to be cumulative.

In cities, we covet the notion that the constituent villages cause interference with their even and relentless spread. Even the straightness of the ceremonial street leading to the palace is tolerated for little more than half a kilometer.

Schlossgarten, Würzburg. Multiple extrusions of vegetation.

I can laugh at all this, but I am the child of such a culture. So I can enjoy the occasional ride down several kilometers of highway in Buenos Aires that announces Argentina's freedom from the Spanish crown, or the centrifugal power of l'Étoile in Paris, but instinctively find them somewhat abstract—even artificial. Not really of the soul or the grain of the city. I respond far more to an ambiguous clustering such as an avenue that winds around a hill and is lost to view much of the time. I am more intrigued by the pile of buildings that must cluster around such a route but only reveal its physiognomy at close quarters. Strangely, people are probably more affected by the mysteries that it might contain than by its availability as a balanced or revealed set piece.

At Würzburg in central Germany, the grounds of the Schloss contain a formal garden, articulated by quarter circles of paths and vegetation that exist in eleven strips: gravel paths, bushes, lawns, trees, paths again, a balustrade, lawn, trees, bushes . . . and more. Without the geometry of route, this sophisticated palette would be inarticulate, yet it remains as much an essay in hierarchy and control as in delight. More modest but more intriguing are the "greenways" that riddle the streets of Letchworth. As a child of twelve and thirteen, I happened to live there, dimly aware that it was a special town: in fact, it was the first Garden City designed by Parker and Unwin and directly informed by Ebenezer Howard's ideas. These protected paths (of considerable width) are well vegetated by the growth of private gardens on either side. Perhaps they were an inspiration for the greenways suggested in the 1970s by Alison and Peter Smithson. I certainly borrowed from their designs—though by then they were bent and distorted—in my **Layer City** and interpreted them as vegetated swathes.

To what extent the bending and twisting is meant as a symbol of inhibition, escape, or romance and to what extent it is offered as a direct counterpoint to a rectilinear road system is a moot point. Le Corbusier himself in his city projects, from Le Plan Voisin to Chandigarh, offers an image of trees as a rather spongy, linear element, able to contrast with the hard geometry of the roads and buildings. In the nineteenth-century villa tradition of England or Germany, it is the private garden that is presumed to be the sponge into which the villa itself might be all but lost so that it might escape the dominance of the supporting road.

Yet in all these examples, the road pattern stems directly from a master plan, some fragmentary memory of such a plan, or elsewhere, a piece of hard-nosed development mathematics. Beyond this, it is the task of the gardener or architect to continue in like manner down the scale, or chose to localize: to defy or escape the tyranny of predictable geometry. Time will then act as an ally and encourage the wayward elements to develop idiosyncrasies: walls decaying or becoming overgrown, the paths into them lost.

Hidden Systems

More intriguing is the loose network of routes and connections that underpin some of the older Oxford or Cambridge colleges, since they do not have a single set of relationships with the enclosing buildings or patches of space. A route may hug a wall, then dart across space, pass through a building, then hug three sides of a quadrangle, only to pass through another building (but in a different manner than before). The act of delving thus seems to contradict any hierarchic view of route dependency. There is much that appears to link this to the use of route in some of the Japanese gardens of Kyoto. There, the highly developed language of symbol and ritual is less prosaic than in England: it is played out through a progression of ritualistic or symbolic moments that have formal presence, too. The tea ceremony pavilion will have a directional focus toward the particular mound, tree, bridge, or lantern, and the path between them may be wayward but in the end will lead to the next "moment." As in England, the use of decoy, tease, ambiguity, and the gentle, subtle coercions that lead the wanderer in a certain direction is combined with understated heroics, seen in the scale and delicacy of the built objects. A circuit of the Rioanji Gardens in Kyoto or of Kent's Rousham gardens in Oxfordshire (and of many other pairings of the progression through Japanese and English gardens) will reveal an uncanny similarity of design psychology coming from both countries.

It is as if a series of scenes in a prearranged life history were to be enacted over a prearranged sequence of spaces, allied of course to a series of preferred vistas or *observations* along the way. Such an approach suits cultures that have a healthy and quizzical detachment from the continental core: Japan from China, England from mainland Europe. Both proud, wayward, indulgent, aware of tradition but always secretly at play. Ascribing certain codified aspects of that play to conditions where those with power, money, and influence could enclose pieces of land and set up private worlds has been the basis for a culture that continues alongside the more Classical interpretation of civilization as the corollary of Order. The small private garden is its progeny. Much of my work is part of this anti-Classical culture and finds its material from the episodic and nearly forgotten. The key thing is for it not to develop into coyness or artiness, not to become deliberately silly. In fact, to be the interpretation of a larger set of ideas, but not a large set of dogmatic pieces.

Arcadia A, the first statement in the Arcadia series of 1976, takes a row of predesigned houses (from Cook and Hawley's Via Appia House of the previous year) and suggests that the disintegrative part of them (the grotto at Via Appia) is the beginning of a secret garden where some (but not all) trees are inhabitable. Some (but not all) hedges are apartments. One end of the garden is bland and the other romantic. The whole episode bounded by a substantial wall. As an early piece, it sets up the icons simply: the tree as nontree, the house as nonhouse, the garden as simple progression. The garden wall is such a characteristic symbol of an English tradition of independence *and* secrecy. The aim of Arcadia at this stage is quite content to be the playing-out-of-little-world of the garden tradition.

The first stage of **Layer City**, seen in Chapter 1, is probably a direct extension of the same idea. The garden wall has disappeared. The hedges, having been allowed to reside inside the Shadow House, are now emancipated and ready to take on the role of making urban space. In the elevation drawing on page 13 there is a subconscious quotation from the grotto part of **Arcadia A**, and the swathes are themselves a case of containment existing in order to permit something potentially wild that can grow and run within the netting.

Shugakuin gardens, Kyoto. The meandering route.

Shugakuin gardens, Kyoto. Lake and bridge as "posed" landscape.

Shugakuin gardens, Kyoto, in context with afforested mountains behind.

Katsura gardens, Kyoto.

ARCADIA A
(Peter Cook, 1981)
This generic project incorporates several ideas that are reexamined in later work: the hedge house, the structured vegetation screen, the orchard, the tree-as-house, the translucency-to-solidity merging skin, and so on.

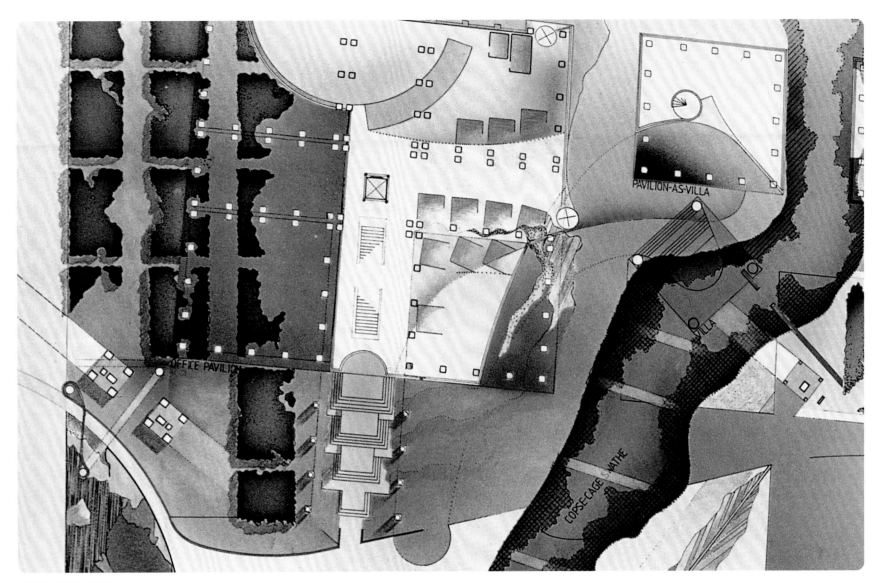

LAYER CITY, DETAIL
(Peter Cook, 1981)

Berlin: White Rooms and Sequences

As a manifestation of magnificently and unashamedly bourgeois instincts, the Kurfurstendamm and the area around it interpreted the German block of apartments on a grander scale than anywhere else except Vienna. Not only are the porches to some of the buildings of the scale of a small chapel, but they are equally endowed with gravitas. The apartments themselves contain the principal salons on the street frontage and then commence that game of corridor as one link and wide interconnecting doors to the next salon as the other. In some of these apartments it repeats and repeats. Eventually you embark on the trail of lesser rooms off the corridor. I know of apartments that continue far down one side and turn around the far corner. Somewhere, there must be one with a string of rooms interconnected right round the block. Our normal notion of a "flat" or of a "room" is seriously challenged by such generosity. For once, the act of living in the heart of the city can be extended and relaxed by space, a real range of light conditions and courtyards of such lush vegetation that a whole spectrum of magnificence has been sustained.

Unlike the Japanese and English mystery or privacy, these courtyards are communal in every sense: the *totality* of the rich patch of garden is essentially an urban statement (except that it is reserved for those permitted to enter the block). The offering is of a certain level of completeness, it is unashamedly large, and the formula is simple: *block-or-court*. No compromise.

Way-Out-West Berlin

Such élan as I have described for the old courts of the turn of the nineteenth and twentieth centuries is sustained for nearly two kilometers. Kurfurstendamm starts to quiet down after the Schaubuhne, and then at the little lake called Halensee it just peters out. There is a highway intersection and a general mishmash of scattered buildings and little else. This puzzled me for years. No doubt there is some history of bombing, split ownership, or maybe lack of "steam"? In 1988 I took up the implied challenge: I would complete the Kurfurstendamm, or rather, give it a culmination. I would challenge it with another heroic arcadia—perhaps of equal but more ironic bourgeois instincts? (Berlin was at that time still divided.) The K'damm was very much the symbol of West Berlin, and my chosen location at the *West of the West*.

A curious patch of forgotten land swings around the back of the Halensee. The lake itself is still flanked by villas and has a fin-de-siècle atmosphere that can be captured on a narrow-angle lens. But a viciously noisy autobahn interchange is just off-camera in one direction, and a brooding piece of railway land lies in the other. Ramshackle brick buildings remain from another time. On this site I set up a West to announce the West: *a piece of Americana*. Of course, you have to be careful with the English when they quote America. For the Archigram generation that came after the Independent Group, America was pop, it was space, it was all those things that Richard Hamilton identifies in his 1956 collage *Just What Is It That Makes Today's Homes So Different, So Appealing?* The muscle man, the tin of ham, the general sense of artificiality. Within the Halensee vacuum I thus imported a little piece of America. Clearly following the orthodox method. Clearly establishing an American grid into which blocks of circumspect and revenue-gathering architecture could be made. A sequence could then be predicted.

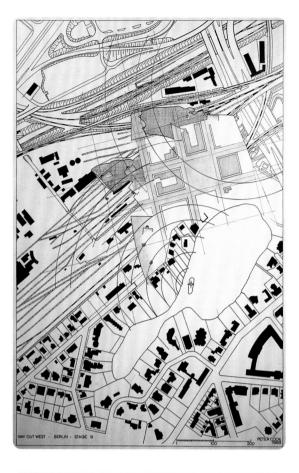

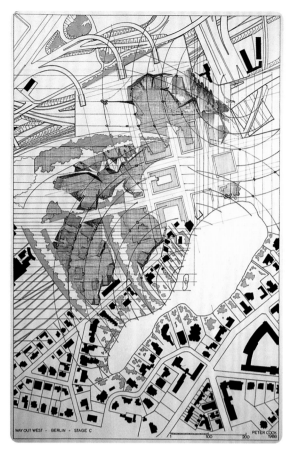

WAY-OUT-WEST BERLIN
(Peter Cook, 1988)
Left: Plan, early stage.
Right: Plan, developing stage.

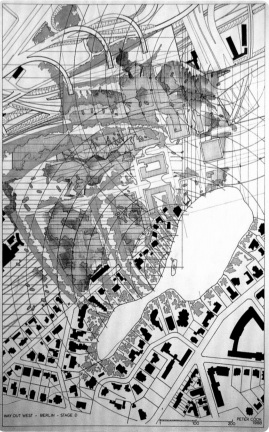

WAY-OUT-WEST BERLIN
Left: Plan, later developing stage.
Right: Plan, highly developed stage.

WAY-OUT-WEST BERLIN
Detail, the gyratory garden knits between two typical pieces of building at the midstage of development.

WAY-OUT-WEST BERLIN
Elevation, the square during metamorphosis.

This type of project occurs in my work every five years or so. In early lectures I would talk about "metamorphosis"—and I still do. Addhox, an English suburban story, was drawn in 1970, the Urban Mark in 1972. In their conception, they rarely have a fully worked out scenario. I try to let the *tendency* of the thing interact with odd concentration points that occur along the way as I am drawing. These points may fizzle out or may well become kernels of a major feature in the next stage. The attempt—and the fascination—is to reproduce creatively the vagaries of growth and change as they seem to be. Few buildings in London or Berlin are used as they were designed, and urban progress is an unpredictable collage. So with **Way-Out-West Berlin** I had to establish a recognizable baseline. A square occupies one patch. A high-rise the next, around them some medium-high commercial blocks in well-mannered downtown architecture: something that SOM or I. M. Pei might do.

Almost immediately, though, the plot thickens. A counteraction is set up. Two points are taken as generators. One is the tiny island that sits in the Halensee, concentrating the spirit of Arcadia, of gentle Berlin. From this focus there are rotating waves of gentle escape that will develop as greenswards. The other point is the geometric center of the autobahn intersection. Symbol of vicious, uncaring, dynamic, determined *artificiality*. All that the Halensee is not. The waves sent from here are more aggressive, more in the nature of germs than gentle wafts. The germs turn out to be parasites that will find interest in the well-mannered blocks.

As in other metamorphic projects, the early stages are critical. Too much drama too soon just looks like confrontation. In order to discover the spirit of the architecture and in order to develop a new language of form, you don't want to lose the subtlety by which one piece of substance starts to ameliorate another or the way in which certain types of distortion reach a critical point in the process and just need to stop. As a trajectory builds up, the drama may appear to have increased, because the forms are unusual, but it is in those early, tweaky stages that the audacity of the idea must lie.

The alternative waves of incursion have very different origins. If the wafts draw from a long series of sweet parks remembered as a child, gardens remembered in the company of friends, and month-by-month reflection on the differences or similarities between London's squares or the green strips that lie between Ernst May's Frankfurt Siedlungen blocks; then, dare one say, it's the easier move. But what of the curious, plantlike bugs that begin to crawl up the calm façades and start to breed a form—a "growth," in fact—that seeps insidiously up and down the surface and creeps around, distorting the very structure of the buildings. The origins of these lie partly in my fascination with the formal implications of "metamorphosis," referred to very often in my lectures of the 1970s, partly in conversations with colleagues and students about the implications of nano-technology, and (not a little) in a boredom with the "straight," the "nice," the "clean" which pervades the contemporary architectural psychology. In other words, they are the necessary irritant that becomes a force.

At which point, the actual name of the project becomes critical. Why *Way-Out*-West Berlin if not from the movies? It is the *real* West, not just that of Europolitics but of that *other* Americana. Creeping out from among the rocks of Arizona or New Mexico is one of God's silliest contraptions: the cactus. Soapy, ungainly, slapped together (a surefire "fail" in a first-year composition exercise). The cactus is ungainly, vegetal, and could, with half a mind, be an alien. Various pods and antennae can develop from this body.

Other overtones are there: the inherited territory was too brooding and too ambiguous not to be toyed with. The rail tracks and a hint of that special nostalgia discussed in Chapter 2 must be there somehow. Thus the "American" grid has been set as a lacework on a deck, below which remain parts of the forgotten Berlin. "Underworld" in both its senses may not be too strong a concept, and surely the remnants begin to empathize with the new mutants. The two detail sections are taken at an early-middle stage and a late-middle stage. It is a workplace with studios and bookstacks and a little corner of underworld below. London's Soho and California finding an agreeably relaxed reception just west of the K'damm. The cactus form outside the window seems cheerful enough in the early stage, but his progeny have overtaken the preppy world of the studio by the next time we take a look. Growths, distortions—new hybrids are at the center of our attention. The discovery of architectural surface and "stuff" is central to my pursuit. Which of them can be caught, which of them becomes the raw material for tectonic progress? For clues, it is necessary to look also at the parts that didn't really change. The elevator shafts, parts of the structure, and much of the underworld. Yet they are not conventional architectural form. The exercise is one of discriminate growth, discriminate distortion, discriminate sterility: all part of the same movement. Architecture that develops out of a dynamic and starts, almost, to breed.

WAY-OUT-WEST BERLIN
A local corner at an earlier stage, with remnants of the
railway beneath, and embryo "cactus" visible.

WAY-OUT-WEST BERLIN
General metamorphosis.

WAY-OUT-WEST BERLIN
The whole square at a later stage of metamorphosis.

As the plans record, there is a progressive move toward the interwoven, but not actually toward chaos, for the fundamental structure remains and absorbs within itself the circular swathe system. As in earlier metamorphic work, the last stage is drawn at a point where the only moves that one might make beyond seem to be either toward total disintegration or backward to a calmer and more rigid territory. Trying to capture the place and the mood is difficult with any design. In this type of change it is necessary to make vignettes. All projects need more and more vignettes, as if they were unconscious moments; yet a contrived piece is rarely unconscious. The nearest drawing may be that of the detail cut through a swathe. The casualness is deliberate. The partially white tiled tunnel under the swathe talks back to the old Berlin of ghosts. The normal-looking trees talk back to other gentler places, while the new vocabulary of tilted glass and cactus derivatives sits there, as if waiting to be challenged.

As with Plug-in City, Urban Mark, Trondheim Library, and the later Veg. House, this project is one that I have drawn on successively. Its progeny are the animal-vegetable elements that quietly creep around the corners of the Breitscheidplatz or become a key energizer in the Finchley Road piece (Chapter 5). The tower in **Way-Out-West** remains a test piece that still contains embryos for future use, particularly in setting out the relationship between fixed space and extendable space.

The Cutting of Swathes—The Transference of Energy

One characteristic of a focal city—London, Tokyo, or Paris—is the incursion of long-distance paths through its crust. We hear the regular sound of trains and vehicles, of energy being pumped into it. And whether they are tourists, commuters, immigrants, or those returning, their energetic focus is on the point of arrival. Then they will disperse and act. Yet foxes reach the inner parts of London along the *edges* of those same paths, as do wildflowers, as do remnants of a time-warped world. If the fascination of the site behind the Halensee in Berlin might have been encouraged by impressionable memories of Christopher Isherwood or Bertolt Brecht, what could be the fascination of Willesden Junction, of the abandoned railway that skirts the hills of North London's Alexandra Palace, or all those small strips of allotments where the only real action is the planting of carrot seeds?

The leapfrog of energy is too simple, for there is a drag effect upon these paths. If the airplane flight path that is computer-controlled represents late-twentieth-century culture, the motorway a mid-twentieth-century technology, and the rail track a late-nineteenth-century experience, then surely these accompanying strips are lodged somewhere in the early nineteenth century. So, ironically, we can combine two seemingly contrary phenomena: the private walled garden containing the most cherished plants and the most elegant escape from the e-mail and the boardroom is selective calm, but the dank strip of railway land lies as an unkempt reminder of *unselective slack*. Together, they are a force that checks our insistence upon hard building, hard alignment, hard surfaces as the necessary representation of the urban state. Jumping out from both conditions and morphing them seems possible. Springing them upon and within and through and *out from* the built building seems exciting.

REAL CITY: FRANKFURT
(Peter Cook, 1986)
Plan, insertion of "avenues" and "villas" on the edge of Offenbach.

REAL CITY: FRANKFURT
Plan, avenue with villas, backyard industry, and market-gardens.

With the **Finchley Road** projects in Chapter 5 we shall encounter some buildings that enjoy coursing along such strips. In the **Veg. House** we shall become involved in the reinvention of the garden, and in the **Super-Houston** work we shall even attempt the reinvention—in a way—of both. Meanwhile, there had already been the attempt to create this same nether-world in **Arcadia City**. Behind the deliberately tough and hard-nosed Lofts area was a casual disintegration toward a rough-and-tumble world of gardens and undefined riverside land. The hard street in front was necessary, perhaps, in order to trigger the stage-by-stage process and to deny, by its toughness, just how far that process might go.

The strips of land suggested for **Real City** are already more energetically focused. It is a project for the intensification of Frankfurt. Already a city of opportunism and trade, it was never the seat of any prince or duke with the type of circumstantial growth that is easily recognized by someone who grew up and studied the growth motives of English provincial towns. So its 1980s aspirations to become a world city touched a nerve. Frankfurt itself is relatively small and surrounded by a myriad of smaller and fiendishly independent towns, of which the nearest is Offenbach. If stature is what it wants, then surely it must become a *real city*. It must grow and create great avenues with great villas inhabiting them as in the great cities of the last two hundred years. It is an interpretation that breaks the predictable image that we might otherwise borrow from Brussels or Madrid.

In the project, the avenues, placed between Frankfurt and Offenbach, intensify the network of direct routes and run between existing node points: so far an orthodox move. The "villas" are actually apartment blocks and stand at an ample distance from each other: still pretty orthodox. The land between is a deliberate combination of recreational garden and intense cultivation for fruit and vegetables: appropriate in an area that was full of orchards until well into the twentieth century. In among this we plant many small buildings—sheds and laboratories, high tech, low tech, general-purpose. From the tradition of backyard industry comes a delightful and opportunist frontyard activity. The buildings folded into the gardens. So what of the villas themselves? They, too, become opportunist: a simple frame made of thrown-out materials: old bits of windows and crushed cars that are then cemented in as part of a great hulk, a frame of elevator shafts and fire corridors, with the offer of filling it left to anyone who opts in.

How might one combine the benefits of the grandeur that I saw in the Kurfurstendamm apartments with the casualness and enterprise implied by people coming and going in a late-twentieth-century way: adding on any kind of infill and leaving any kind of surface? Either by suggesting a real free-for-all—even some "hippie" dwellings—or by using the hulk as the basis for a series of essays in housing. The vegetated block, the urbane block, the intricate block. And the line of sight from these blocks? Inevitably, one that is absorbed by groupings of spongy trees.

What, then, is the urban space that signifies? Is it the chamber, the court, the tracing of the surface, or the territory of escape? Even if one has a passing preference for one of these, the question remains: what is it that we see? Even if one can answer this, a further question still remains: does what we see really reveal the spirit of the place or merely a reference to it, leaving us to make the act of discovery?

REAL CITY: FRANKFURT. THE HULK
A basic, cheap mass-core for a villa.

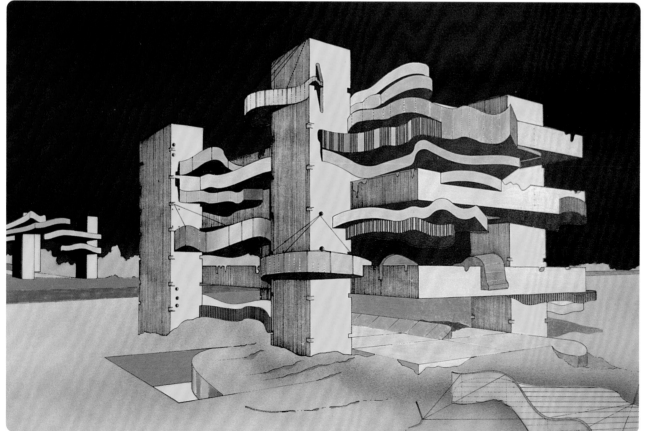

REAL CITY: FRANKFURT
The "hulk" with minimal additions for occupation.

Opposite:
REAL CITY: FRANKFURT
A villa (developed hulk) interpreted as Veg.-Villa.

4

THE CITY OF SURPRISE

A Question of Detachment

Perhaps there are two types of urban tyranny: blind arrogance or deadly acquiescence. For a designer, especially one who works with other people, it is necessary to create an atmosphere of intensity around the current project. Just as an actor who gradually begins to grow into the character he will play, to behave or look like him in day-to-day life, so the architect will begin to see significance *for the scheme* in otherwise commonplace phenomena. One homes in on a selective view of the world. One drives past a bridge, and something in its structure is *of the scheme*. One glimpses a corner at the far end of a shop, and it has something to do with a potential space *within the scheme*. One sees a silhouette at a certain moment in the evening and it conjures up a momentary vision *of the profile of the scheme.* This form of obsession is related to concentration, but because a building is a contributory force to a world that exists, it must draw from that world in order to put something into it.

Yet overlaid upon this process of conscious and unconscious observation there is the ego, the hypothesis, the internal dynamic. There is a certain collective power in the world of young, talented, ambitious students and their wound-up, brilliant, concentrated teachers, along with all their frustrated, oblique, imaginative friends. This power drives architecture forward: you can find few innovative architects who are not, at some time, teaching. There is an elite that lectures and publishes: their buildings are inevitably icons. These icons, when considered together, create a chain dynamic. Fashion? Sometimes. Anticipation of what will become part of the ongoing vernacular? Often.

The difficult question is now raised: how valid is it for architecture to have its own culture? Its own self-satisfying and self-contained art form? Or is its proper place as a domestic art, as a service? Can it have a detached development, such as music, which touches the public nerve only via a combination of acknowledged code mixed with emotional release? The concert hall on the one hand and the shepherd's whistle on the other. Painting comes closer to the dilemma, since it sometimes depicts reality—or degrees of reality. At which point it might offer comment. It might conjure up an alternative view of life—or even of space. My own generation is that of film and television. Here the issue intensifies: these genres hardly exist outside the territory of reflection, the world played back to the world. Yet it is precisely at this point that the act of not playing back the *actual* world is possible. And can be imperceptible. The film and the building are threatening and threatened.

If you saw a film with a sinister take on life, the next day you might feel a certain sense of unease. If you experienced a building that did not reveal ordinary and predictable space, your response to old familiar places might be either relief or frustration.

It has been the role of so-called functionalism to bring such issues to the fore. Inevitably allied to the socialist ideal, it wedded the morality of social reality or responsibility to that of material honesty and things-being-what-they-are. Under such a stricture—and functional criteria are still the link between "high" architecture and the world outside—Modern architecture began to set up all sorts of codes representing honesty. *What you see is what you get:* a leg is a leg, a top is a top. This was perhaps parallel to the down-home values of the settler in a new country. Before long, however, functionalism could begin to be abstracted and brought to a certain code of expressionism. A certain kind of leg was more definitively "about being a leg" and a certain top "speaks to us of top." In a sense, architecture found its way back to the condition of an art form.

The Pompidou Effect and the Blue Whale

There was the usual outcry when Piano and Rogers's building for the Place Beaubourg in Paris was revealed. Defenders automatically cited the Eiffel Tower as proof that Paris could deal with innovative metal icons. But the tower is detached from the urban grain, seen at a distance in a park. Beaubourg was inserted within the grain and more threatening because it could be offered, not as a toy or an obelisk, but as an alternative building. In its earlier versions it might have been even more challenging, as it was intended to have more working parts and vast moving-media projections on its flanks. A piece of alternative city is being offered. Its philosophy shares that of my Plug-in City and much of Cedric Price's Fun Palace (as well as developing some of the components of them both). A response to the emancipation of people's activity and time in the twentieth century, a parallel response to the possibilities offered by technology. Lovers of Paris as a built museum wrung their hands and were totally unprepared for the building's unmitigated success. The public arena of the Place Beaubourg, its flanking chain of panoramic escalators, and the airy rooftop views acted as a palliative to the very new architecture.

After a while, such new architecture became associated in the popular mind with such offerings. The museum need not remain a mausoleum for culture; the form of a public building need no longer send out signals that it is competing, on behalf of the public, with the palace. (That game was played out in nineteenth-century cities.)

The Centre Pompidou on the Place Beaubourg, Paris.
(Renzo Piano and Richard Rogers, 1972-77)

Pacific Design Center, "the Blue Whale," West
Hollywood. (Cesar Pelli, 1967)

It suggested that a city as large, as confident, and as dense as Paris could absorb an element of surprise. This makes the condition of the Pacific Design Center in Los Angeles even more intriguing, for if that city is quite large and confident, in its own way, it is certainly not dense. Furthermore, in the 1970s the city's attitude toward institutions was still ambiguous. Most of its inhabitants had fled from the more uptight parts of Europe or the eastern half of the United States and existed without the public squares, palaces, or cultural basilicas of the old cities. The Griffith Park Observatory was the nearest thing to a popular built icon because of its location. The County Art Museum and the City Library were flung far apart, and when proposed, the Design Center seemed unlikely to upset the calm.

Institutionally, it was a far cry from the European model: a conglomeration of rentable spaces within a block located in the particularly low-density subcity of West Hollywood, a location for designers and the world of Camp. The blue glass block, with its single half-tube running along the roof, did something that no other building in Southern California had achieved at the time: it identified the place as a large and complete icon. The trick, then, was that its glass, when seen at certain angles, reflected the whole picture of West Hollywood itself. No copies of the formula have succeeded as well. In one move it established Los Angeles as a world city with the first of many palaces. This suggests, of course, that all cities need major icons and that these should be identifiable and easy to describe as well as easy to find.

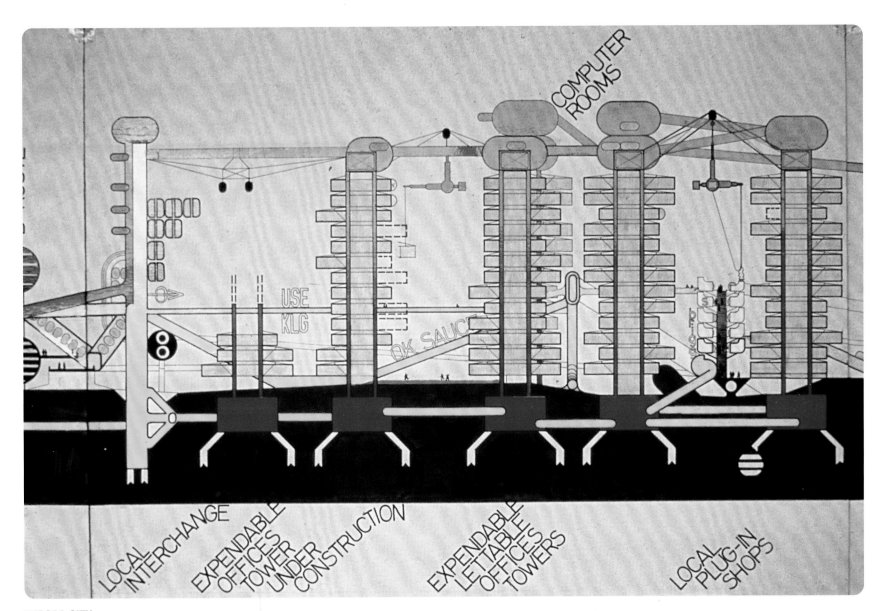

EUROPA CITY
(Peter Cook, 1963–64)
A schematic precursor of the Plug-in City.

St. Pancras station, London: the giant shed looms up out of an urban landscape.

King's Cross station, London: action within the giant shed.

Tel Aviv bus station (Ram Karmi, 1985–95).

Great Sheds

Already in the eighteenth century and certainly by the middle of the nineteenth, London was large and active enough to withstand the imposition of a second generation of powerful buildings to follow the churches and palaces. These came, however, through the demands of industry or trade and the power of the railway. Maps can most easily expose the violence with which the establishment of Smithfield Market, Spitalfields Market, or Billingsgate took place: certainly the coagulated villages that existed around them took giant knocks. The great railway stations, too, were placed in edge conditions that nonetheless contained houses.

The city regrouped itself after these incursions, with some strange urban acrobatics around the paths of the railways. Viaducts, in particular, offered me the clues of another physiognomy that I could develop in the early stages of **Plug-in City**: unlike the areas of Southwark, where the viaducts leave opportunities only for daredevils to fit buildings into impossible, small, triangular sites, in my plan the viaduct was the generator of the buildings and also, of course, the path along which the replacement parts of those buildings could be made.

If castles so often made the first move in the process of establishing medieval and Renaissance cities, this fact was progressively forgotten in the eighteenth and nineteenth centuries, when steady augmentation was the game. Swathes of homogeneity began to grow and exude calm. The incursion of a giant element could not interfere with the basic trend but could have a perverse and ultimately positive effect. After the market came the waves of daily activity, the reconstitution of the village, now a working part of a complex series of systems. After the station, even more waves of activity and the accelerated weaving of town along and around it. In London, the stations ranged along the strip of Paddington, Marylebone, Euston, St. Pancras, and King's Cross, offering a scaled-up version of the towers and ramparts of a city edge.

Penn Station sets its great foot into Manhattan only to announce the presence of New Jersey, Pennsylvania, and points south, but what an announcement. It could not do the job better if it were a deep piece of the Hudson cut in as a bay. It only engages at the front end. The city works around it. In an even more extraordinary way, the elevated concrete mass of the Tel Aviv bus station steps on to the city and hardly engages at all. In scale, a much greater piece than the London markets and stations, it is ignored by all but the poorest inhabitants and is full of unoccupied space. A megastructure that is 50 percent alive within a 120 percent city.

Mere contrariness is not enough. If the City of Surprise is positive, that which surprises must have an engaging personality.

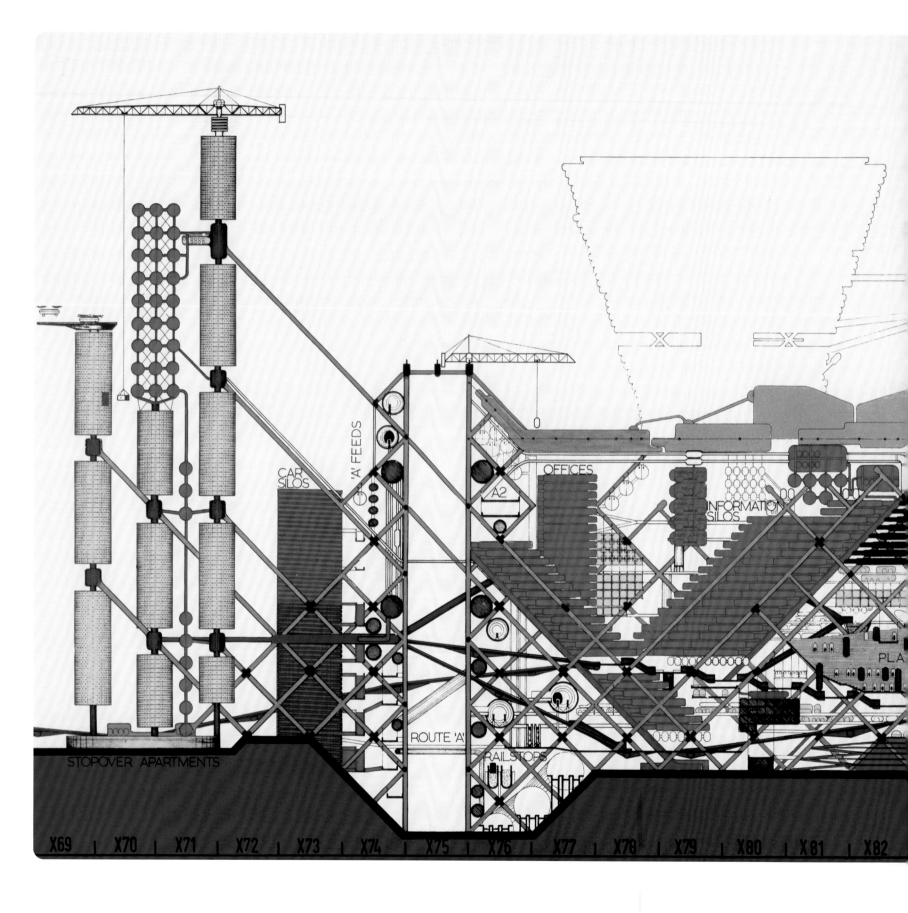

STOPOVER APARTMENTS

CAR SILOS

'A' FEEDS

A2

OFFICES

INFORMATION SILOS

PLA

ROUTE 'A'

RAILSTOPS

X69   X70   X71   X72   X73   X74   X75   X76   X77   X78   X79   X80   X81   X82

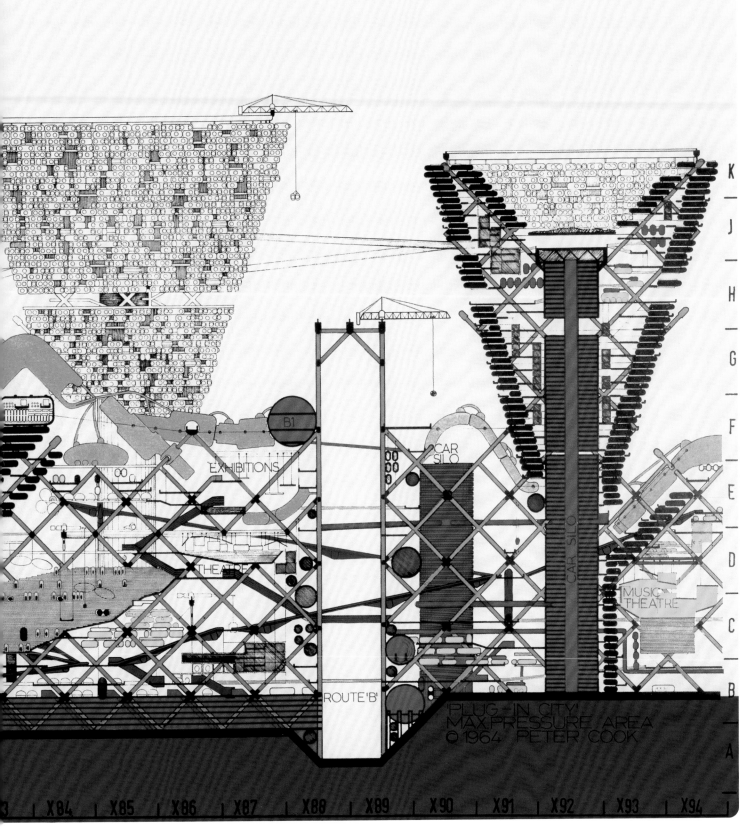

EXHIBITIONS

CAR SILO

THEATRE

MUSIC
THEATRE

CAR SILO

ROUTE 'B'

B1

PLUG-IN CITY:
MAX PRESSURE AREA
© 1964   PETER COOK

K
J
H
G
F
E
D
C
B
A

3 | X84 | X85 | X86 | X87 | X88 | X89 | X90 | X91 | X92 | X93 | X94 |

Detached Mystery

Two further examples intrigue me because they seem to break every rule. First, "the white thing behind Oslo." Such would have been my description in the summer of 1968 as I tried to get my first bearings in a city that has subsequently become one of my favorite haunts. As we have already noted, hills rise up out of the fjord and hard buildings are gradually replaced by soft buildings and then partially hidden buildings as you climb upward. Among the softest and most hidden, near the skyline, is the *White Thing*. Not even a pure shape—not a slab or tower, not a chunk or a heap. It can be seen as solid, featureless, scaleless, and slightly lurching. Even when explained as a functioning object, the relationship of the main action to the shape seems vague.

Before further explanation, it is enjoyable to hold on to this predicament for a moment, especially when so much other architecture is overt, featured, conglomerate, or consequent. My delight is in a great white Thing up there in the nowhere.

Well, it is the Olympic ski slope, from the 1950s. When seen at close quarters, it has seats, handrails, doors, and other substantial features. Sure, it's big and white but it no longer holds much interest for me. In my ever-present dream that architecture can be almost ethereal I want there to be more objects of mystery, but also of a detached reality, strewn around a city so that the real, busy, circumstantial world can enjoy them and engage with them but only intermittently—almost surreptitiously. Peasants and farmers were not necessarily allowed to enter the great castle up on the hill but knew it was there, ready to give them support at the right moment.

Not exactly following the same logic but in an even more curious relationship to their context are the three concrete towers established by the German military as they organized themselves in Vienna at the end of the 1930s. Whether or not the Viennese were receptive to the idea of the greater Reich, these things must have seemed surprising—if not gross—in the context of a city that had been rarely interfered with. They must have seemed offensive in their lack of detail—just giant shafts of raw concrete and giant semicircular pads aloft, to take unseen gun emplacements. They must have seemed alien in their total detachment

The Olympic ski jump on Holmenkollern, Oslo.

World War II gun tower, 6th district, Vienna.

Sheffield City Hall.

from the streets and doorways around them, speaking with an unexpected force to an unknown adversary. As total as Oslo's ski jump, if hardly as benign.

In all this, our ideas of congruity are mixed with our assumptions about the spirit of a place. The parallel ideas about the role played by buildings within a city are also there to be clarified. It is in some ways a question of emancipation.

So far as we can tell, the idea of power, influence, and mandate for the very few was accepted by the majority in medieval times, open to modest infiltration in the age of Enlightenment, and progressively infiltrated up to the early twentieth century, when the proletariat was finally recognized as a driving force. As always, architecture merely followed the pattern. Castles and cathedrals were the manifestation of military and religious power. Palaces and colleges were the repositories of informed exchange. City halls and bathhouses the mirror of public patronage and paternalism. So far, they successively borrowed from the previous symbolism of detachment. As architecture they had to be special: Alexandra Palace on a north London hilltop was a "palace of the people" (perhaps a forerunner of the Russian workers' clubs of the 1920s). Necessarily grandiose, even of exaggerated scale. The New York Public Library was the royal palace that such a city could never have. The nineteenth-century town halls of industrial cities strived further and further to convince their citizens that they were represented by an architecture of intricate quality. Leeds vied with Manchester, and in the twentieth century Stockholm with Oslo.

The Modernist ethic infiltrated this pattern by homogenizing the expressionistic code of almost all types of building. A city hall could be regarded as a large secretariat and therefore represented by *more* lines of window, rather than fewer. Ceremony could be reduced, domes and porticoes were not needed as markers: the role of the heroic building that had somehow survived from castle to post office became questionable.

A final tyranny was absorbed: the combination of populism and revivalism, so that major buildings in certain cities began to lose themselves in a commonplace mulch of endless modest objects.

The Decision to Detach

My own work has consciously flown in the face of such thinking, especially a part of the **Arcadia** project called the **Sleek Corner.** It came very quickly, more an image than a planned-out design. In my mind it was unusually vehement, almost aggressive. A shrill cry against the current hair-shirt attitude toward architecture in some English circles (against brown rice and tweedy surfaces). Rhetorically artificial, knowingly contemporary, deliberately sleek. The artificiality was personified by very unnatural colors—certainly nothing reminiscent of brick, stone, or wood; if built, then it would certainly involve many chemicals and processed techniques. But what of the green growths creeping up from the rear? And what of the sudden outburst of irrelevant bubbles? These had a deliberate part to play in the reinforcement of the "sleek" statement. The growing vegetation threatened only slightly and could easily be checked and trapped by the inhospitable glassy surface. The bubbles were a direct quotation of the "beauty spots" that coquettes, the highly powdered heroines of eighteenth-century Restoration comedy, applied to their faces. The purpose of these spots was to call attention to the total perfection of the beautified face!

In a project that posed the various districts as stark alternatives to one another, Sleek Corner acted as an extreme position of both viciousness and blandness. This is something that I have not frequently repeated, but it was quite exhilarating at the time.

**ARCADIA, THE SLEEK CORNER
(Peter Cook, 1978)
Created for the Sponge project, the Sleek Corner was appropriated for Arcadia City. It implies a totally artificial world in contradistinction to the romanticism of the Arcadian countryside.**

An earlier building, the project for the **Trondheim Library** in Norway, was equally sleek but much more tricky in its ways of detachment from the mode of its city and always conscious of the characteristics of that city. Developed together with Christine Hawley, it was only our third joint project. Moreover, it was running hard on the back of the **Via Appia House** and shared some of the same thinking on the issue of transparency, translucency, and the deliberate muting of the transmission of form—or silhouette—from within to without. It was to sit between a wide street of colored wooden warehouses—open and reiterative— and a much tighter piece of town on the other three sides with many banks, shops, and an art school.

The library was located in a place accustomed to rain and dark evenings, and many of the users were expected to be people from the nearby university, so we felt that it should be a year-round refuge. Not just for books, but for a whole special world in which reading and research could be an excuse for sitting in a special place. Indeed, two words kept running round our heads: *garden* and *theater*. Perhaps, too, it was the recognition of that special Trondheim room described in the last chapter, where the rest of the surrounding world could be held at bay. Perhaps it was the idea that a big library with several high-profile departments—and thus, several differing types of people—could range around the "garden" of the big lending–reading room. The particularity, the gentleness of this internal world needed to be protected against the weather of middle Norway. Yet the building had to avoid being a fussy object.

Indeed, we enjoyed the idea that all was not what it seemed: from the outside it was a smooth glass object, an extended arcade. If you passed by on the side of the wide street, you would see some shadowy forms silhouetted through the muted glass, but that's all. Around the corner, in a narrow gap between some old shops you would find the entrance to this arcade—quite modest and beckoning you in. You would enter and start to climb slowly and wind round along the arcade, quite soon coming upon a great internal space off to the left. The seven internal "buildings" (the departments of the library) stand around the great space, each with its own character and shape. Moving along the arcade and gradually making your way round the space, you would perceive the seven pieces changing and new aspects of each of them being revealed. In many ways this was a Gothic composition and a Gothic set of sensibilities. Immediate in scale, particular in expression. Yet the exterior remained *smooth and cool*.

This duplicity of message was particularly apt in a city with challenging weather, but the external *hint* of the Gothic was essential in order to avoid blandness. By the same token, an outside form of the same intricacy as the interior would have been too fussy and broken-down, especially in an old city. Out of *respect* for Trondheim, we refused to play any contextual game in terms of style, grain, or force. Yet the shafts of clear light flowing through the gaps between the seven piles remain as a reminder of the scale of the place. The smooth sweep of the glass can be absorbed by sensibilities familiar with long sweeps of water and low sweeps of light on the horizon. It is a city that can handle such a program of gentle surprise.

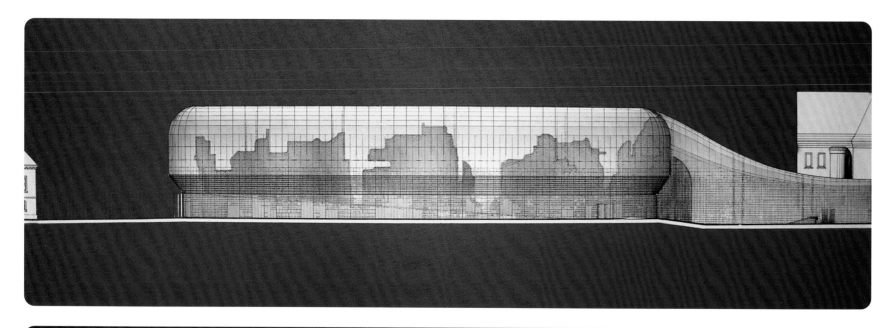

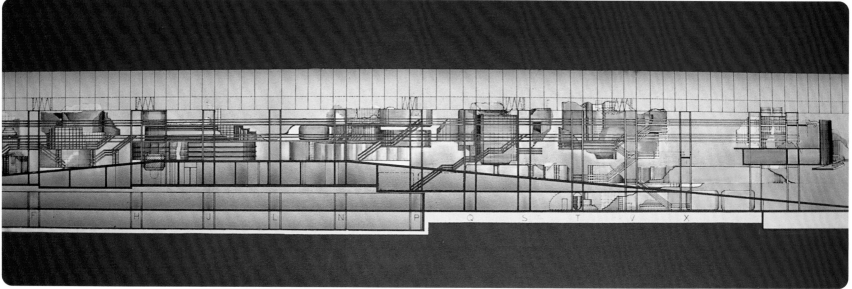

TRONDHEIM LIBRARY, ELEVATION
The interior buildings are shadowy forms within the cocoon of translucent glass.

TRONDHEIM LIBRARY, SECTION
(Peter Cook and Christine Hawley, 1977)
An "unfolded" view of the strip of interior buildings that are protected within the
translucent cocoon and flank the climbing arcade.

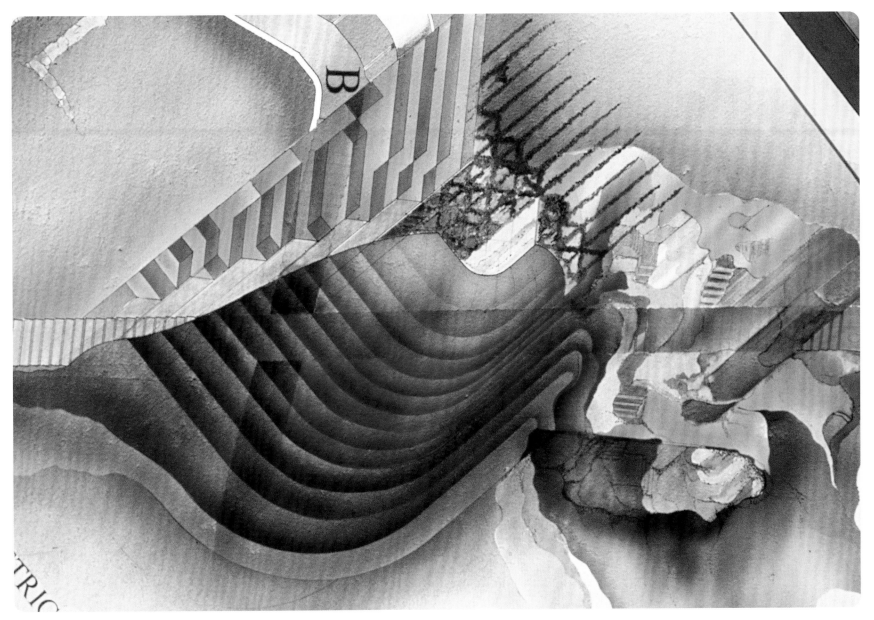

VIA APPIA HOUSE, AXONOMETRIC
(Peter Cook and Christine Hawley, 1976)
A project for the Shinkenchiku house competition, set that year by Richard Meier. Dense-to-translucent, translucent-to-transparent skin gives way to racked vegetation (reused in Arcadia A). Two directions of metamorphosis.

Sleekness returns some twenty-three years later at the **Kunsthaus, Graz**, in another old town and at the opposite corner of Europe. Similarly placed between a wide street (and a river) on the one side and a hug from a clutch of early-nineteenth-century buildings on the other side. Colin Fournier (with whom I had worked on the **Features: Monte Carlo** scheme and the previous Graz **Tongue**) and I developed a knobbly but sleek-skinned cocoon that sits above the ground. As with the Tongue, this form erupts toward the top in a series of large funnels—a clue to the purpose of the building.

The entrance lies under the Eisenes Haus, the earliest cast-iron structure in southern Austria (which we virtually had to reconstruct). From this runs a thin travelator up into the unknown spaces in the skin. Most of it is opaque, but from time to time there are revealing slivers of transparency or hints of the presence of action within. The skin is not glass, as it was at the library, nor are the slivers at Graz as consistent as the general translucency of the Trondheim building, but stranger things appear and disappear within the skin: signs, announcements, short sequences of film or images. They are glimpsed, only to fade away. Much of this is achieved by electrics and electronics, since we use one thousand pixels—each a fluorescent ring that sits behind the Plexiglas skin. This sleek cocoon is a membrane that hints at new and creative activities within, as well as inviting interactive programs and invented programs to animate it. At night, there are revelations (or perhaps they are decoys?). At times parts of the interior can be identified—but never too much. At times the electric image and the shadows between confuse with the sighting of a solid presence. And at some time, even the most passive voyeur must be tempted to glide up into the interior.

At the top of the travelator the story is partially revealed: a large and highly tunable space is the "black box"—a studio for the creation, exhibition, or viewing of electric and electronic art. Ideally, small wheeled rooms, like buses, packed with electronics and projectors, would be guided and parked around the space to make possible almost any setup, as in a TV studio, though at the moment, these have been kicked out of the budget!

Up the second travelator and into a completely different atmosphere—light and airy, with the funnels articulating the space and throwing directed, natural light onto the artworks or installations within. In the tradition of the Kunsthalle, this Kunsthaus is to be the instrument for that quizzical, ironic, but always inventive art that the Austrians encourage. Wandering around this hall, you come upon the occasional funnel that is playing its own quizzical and ironic game, giving an almost theatrical set-piece view of the cute castle on its chunky small mountain, just across the river. Or alternatively, glancing at the onion domes of the old city churches, you are reminded that there were already some bubbly skins there in the eighteenth century.

Above the art and the secret world within the cocoon, there is a long, bean-shaped room that rides across the smooth form of the galleries. Having reached it, you can detach yourself from everything except the view of the city—itself the ultimate "art piece"—seen after a process of optical coercion and atmospheric exhaustion.

Once again, the city has been respected in the sense that our building is prepared to snuggle down into the bosom of the town, but not prepared to pretend that it is in any way typical of it. It is a special instrument. It contains secrets. And since it is more volatile than the Trondheim Library, since it must respond several times a year to the creativity of the artists who make the special world in the black box or the icons within the airy hall, it has to be far more versatile. Perhaps it is a Classical concept, as opposed to the Gothic, with two competing *pianos nobiles,* one above the other.

Two or three surprises, experienced in sequence, or several more, experienced in time?

Graz is not a large city, but one of unusual maturity. Much of it hidden behind the castle and laid out in small clusters that remain remarkably intact. Another challenge is the intriguing recent history of its architectural culture. No other city of its size has generated a definitive (and much discussed) coterie of architects: the Grazer Schule, in its twenty or thirty years, has been responsible for more inventive work than several whole nation-states. Some of these architects were already our good friends, so the challenge of building among them was in our minds, in addition to the challenge of building among intact historical grain. We knew that Gunther Domenig, Volker Giencke, Klaus Kada, and the rest were watching us. We could not mimic their mannerisms but we could give a long, low wink and a long, low gurgle from within the cocoon, knowing that our building is more slithery and more somnambulant than theirs.

KUNSTHAUS, GRAZ
(Peter Cook and Colin Fournier, 2000–)
First Prize in an international competition.
The building is now under construction.
Model, the building in context (January 2001
version).

KUNSTHAUS, GRAZ
Nighttime view.

KUNSTHAUS, GRAZ
Plan of first-floor gallery (black-box condition).

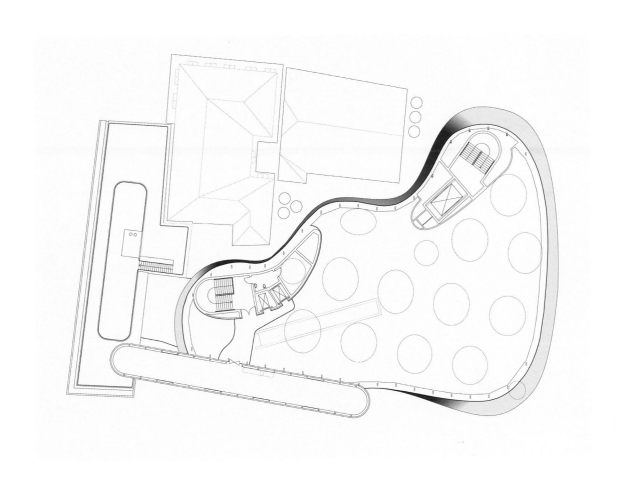

KUNSTHAUS, GRAZ
Plan of ground floor.

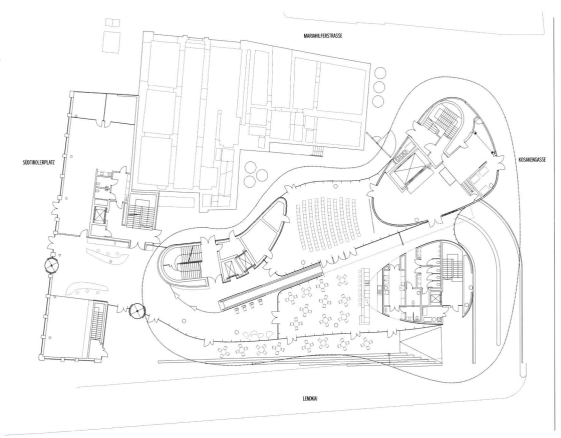

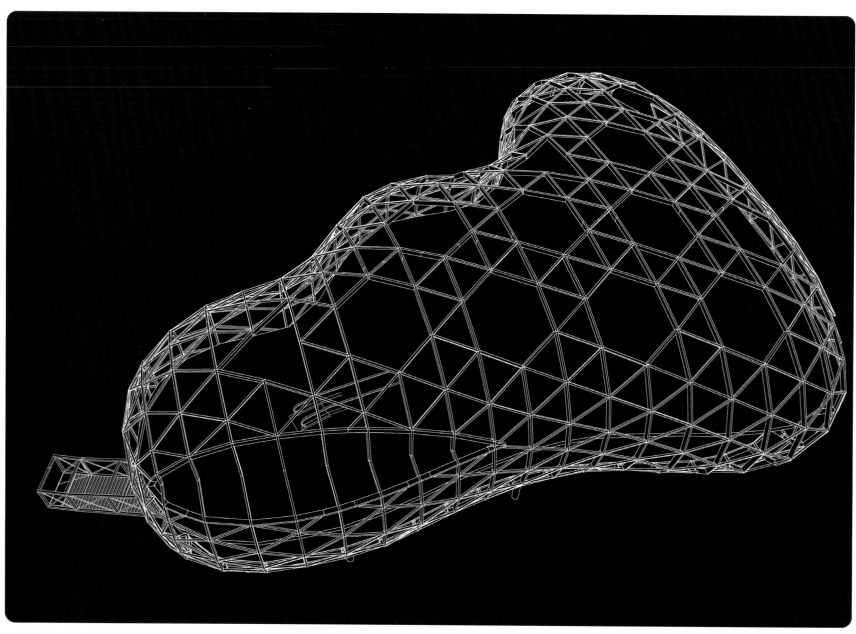

KUNSTHAUS, GRAZ
Structural "cage."

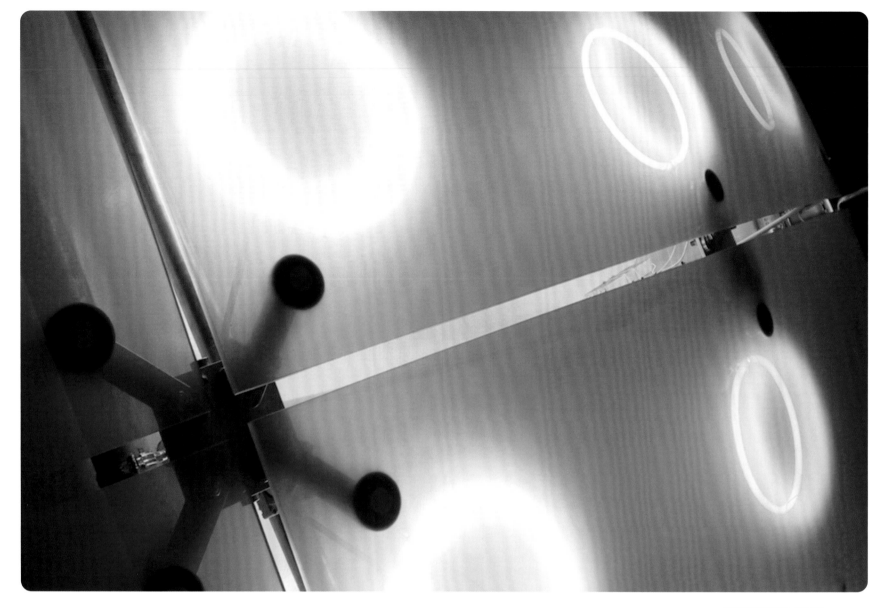

KUNSTHAUS, GRAZ
Detail of skin.

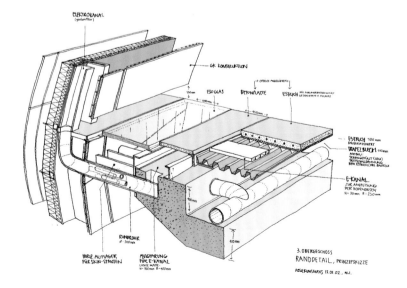

KUNSTHAUS, GRAZ
Section.

KUNSTHAUS, GRAZ, PERSPECTIVE

KUNSTHAUS, GRAZ, SECTION

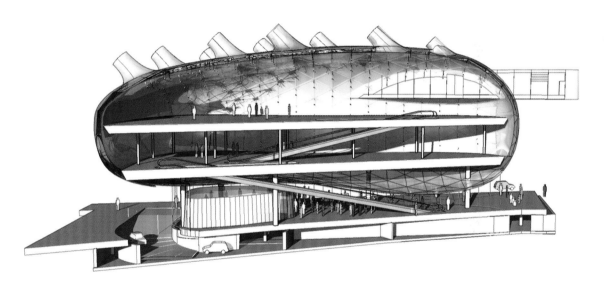

KUNSTHAUS, GRAZ: UPPER-LEVEL INTERIOR
(Computer rendition by Nicola Haines, 2000)

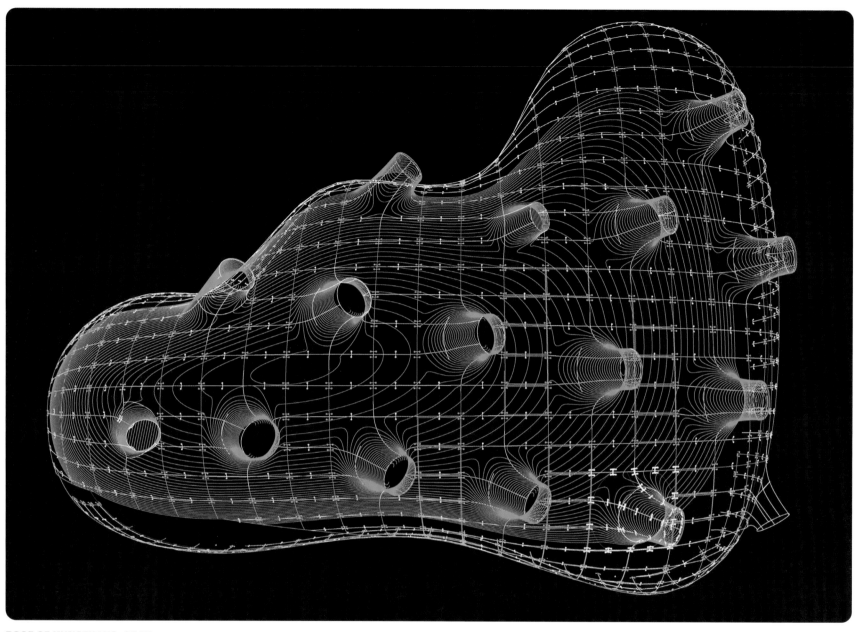

ROOF OF KUNSTHAUS, GRAZ.

Kunsthaus in context, Graz.
(Harry Schiffer, Graz)

Detail, Kunsthaus, Graz.
(Harry Schiffer, Graz)

A Calculated Offense

Long before, I had accepted Brian Appleyard's invitation to draw some ideas about the part of London that lies on the south side of the River Thames, for publication in the London *Times*. It was before the area became touristy, and my target, anyhow, was the deeper zone, some distance from the river.

To be frank, the place caused me that same spurt of frustration that had instigated the Sleek building. Why, oh why, did we waste time on crap? Was it worth preserving what was down there? In a calculated burst of gross political incorrectness, I proposed the idea of flooding a large part of Southwark. A giant lagoon would be surrounded by beaches and resorts. New resort structures and the odd island would be developed. This part of South London might finally be worth a visit!

Since my article appeared in a newspaper famous for apoplectic correspondence, I sat tight and waited for the inevitable splutterings of horror, which obediently came. In reality, I am too much of a softie to really want to drown anyone, yet I'm not sure I can hide my disrespect for tacky pieces of city with lazy, third-rate architecture. Especially in England, we have too much regard for the inconsequential. We preserve far too much. If this project was an angry cry or a letting off of steam, it does by comparison suggest that the Pompidou, the blue whale, the glazed Gothic room, and our blue cocoon are more germinators than predators and, indeed, that they *respect the idea of the city*.

LONDON LAGOON
(Peter Cook, 1984)
The creation of a large lake in Lambeth totally reorients the focus and activities of South London.

5

THE CITY OF INVENTIONS

Airport Observations

As we collect our memories of cities we overlay a combination of responses—to streets and structures, to revelations of space, to episodes and distortions. If we are really enjoying ourselves, it doesn't matter if these get mixed together in an almost unfathomable mulch and we simply carve our way through. Only when making a historical analysis or when making a piece of city design do we seem to prize them all apart again and set parameters for the idea of "building," "site," "mechanism," "fitting," "room," "enclosure," "decorative element," "device." Subconsciously we are recognizing hundreds of years of cultural pressure to place one condition on a higher plane than the other. The avenue above the yard, the gateway above the bay window, the institute above the warehouse, the marketplace above the duck pond, the house above the kiosk.

I would like to invert all this if I could, but I too am the child of that same system of recognition, with a background of processes and references steeped in such values. Even turning them over in the usual way of movement-against-movement—monumentalism replaced by anti-monumentalism or decoration as an antidote to Puritanism—seems even to perpetuate the system. The true act of inversion would be one in which a totally *scrambled* set of artifacts were allowed to take on a totally *random* set of forces. So the act of looking at the cities that I experience, searching for clues, turning these clues into creative fodder, and sending that back again (which is my current strategy) has to resort to some elastic means, and take a look at the edges of the system.

The backside districts of neat cities—such that Leith is to Edinburgh, Vienna outside the Girtel is to the inner city, or Queens is to Manhattan—all give wonderful clues to the real activity of the city away from the smart avenues and an equal clue to the paranoias of the citizens. In the English street tradition, the backsides of houses (in contrast to the circumspect frontages) let everything hang out, including people's real personalities.

So it may be no accident that so many of the references of Russian Constructivist architecture were a Soviet idealization of industrial structures and engineering, as if glamorizing the means of production while simultaneously envying and mocking the power of Western industrial cities through the parts of which they did not boast (but which economically gave them the edge). More recently, through the complex demands of enterprise and the fragmentation of the traditional "workplace" (whether mill, office block, or department store), "backsides" have exploded and their untidy progeny have often landed in scary proximity to the most consumer-friendly features of a city. Architectural neatness is under challenge from this new plague.

For me, such an explosion reaches its weirdest state and its most exciting relationship in one or two very large airports. Let's forget the small, neat ones, but get rummaging around the large, hairy ones—especially those that have been growing over three or even five decades: La Guardia, O'Hare, Heathrow, or Frankfurt. The last two, my own highway markers for the last twenty years, have been continually metamorphosing all that time,

Long Beach, the unsung flank of greater Los Angeles: port, factory, resort, testbed.

Heathrow Airport, London: push-pull, link, fill, swivel, infill.

and not just through the neat addition of whole terminals. More by the continual addition and adaptation of small pieces.

An access finger will be stripped down, doubled in size, and then rerouted. A main passenger artery will dive across a diagonal or be bent around a Z shape into an H shape. A deck will be carved into a void. Another void will be carved into a myriad of rooms. Something will be tacked along the edge. So far, though, this description (reminiscent of the arrangement of the Oxford or Cambridge colleges) is flat and two-dimensional. Once we get into the third dimension, the absurd but fluid magic is open for endless concoctions. Not only have escalators created a true fluidity to people's movement, but every kind of substance can be woven and guided over space—baggage, liquids, machines, air—and the idea of proximity starts to elasticate.

In the airport, circumstance forces improvisation. Speed of interchange means money, and the symbolism of activity—one of the architect's old delights—is severely challenged. We weep a tear over the simultaneous loveliness and rigidity of Saarinen's former TWA terminal at Kennedy; we are already beginning to feel nostalgia toward the first terminal at Charles de Gaulle. In such architecture, the "wrap" was the manifestation, the larger "wrap" represented significant space.

A syndrome that might have come out of São Paulo seems to be involved, and urban infilling, rollovers, skewers-through, or fold-ins mean that every change in traffic can be lurched toward. A terminal sometimes feels like traditional architecture (on the inside, where they want you to look). So new terminologies need to be invented for the new hybrids: how about land-pier, sandwich zone, sponge chamber, route bundle, general-purpose air-conditioned huts, fold-through, zip up? Primitive terminology for items that are anything but primitive. Composite, cutable, munchable materials and plenty of hidden slack through which tubes, belts, or wires can be threaded. Nice engineering and some good glass walling momentarily reassure (or monumentalize), but this misses the point. For here a new architecture is being created and a new model for the city is evolving. You perform an act here and (mysteriously) arrive at another point, where you perform another act but have little idea of hierarchy, orientation, or interval. It becomes rather like the experience of a late-night taxi ride in a strange town.

The city that will sometime develop out of this world will have its antecedents in the crazier parts of the crazier opportunist cities but will more significantly be the child of the amazing range of machines and gizmos that are freely used. The sensors, the spouts, and the folding, stretching, impacting, swinging elements; the imprinted, the simulated, the morphed, the implicit—culminating in an elegantly *gutless* architecture. Full of inventions that started life on the battlefield, the battery farm, the refrigerated hold, the printing press, or the hospital . . . plus some other unlikely breeding grounds for "nice" architecture.

Tel Aviv, crazy city.

Newcastle, city of machined links.

Oporto, crazy city.

Oporto, crazy bits and pieces.

Oporto/Wuppertal: Invention and Surprise

There is a refreshing quality somewhere within this tendency—unsentimental and acquisitive. It takes what it needs and has few cultural prejudices. Most cities that we know take the opposite approach: loading down the daily circumstances with ritual and ritualized buildings. Supposedly this is their charm—but in guidebook terms. So it was refreshing to discover recently a city that has a similar lack of prejudice. Inevitably a "second city" rather than a capital (for capitals are often too self-conscious), it seems to have enjoyed centuries of uninterrupted activity on the edge of Europe, along with a healthy sense of survival. The Portuguese city of Oporto occupies the hillside of an estuary and comfortably wraps itself in and out of civilized vegetation. It offers us warehouses, a cathedral, and many churches tiled in blue and white. But it also offers the richest mix of icons and constructions of any city of its size. The connoisseur will find the local variation on the merchant's house or the fisherman's cottage, but more particularly a nonchalant scattering of 1930s Modernism— almost Belgian in its Deco overtones, workaday Jugendstijl, strange nods in the direction of Scandinavia and England, or Rococo themes from the Iberian interior.

The extent of its richness lies, however, in the less conscious structures. In every street there are naughty corners, absurd outcrops, tin sheds on top of worthy piles, ramshackle (but clever) appendages to already clever buildings. The infrastructure, too, has the same quality, by which a grand avenue will readily give up its ambition and fizzle out into a zigzag, only to start up again. Major activities are "discovered" within the general patchwork of the undulating streets. Shop-fronts of inventive hilarity wink back at shop-fronts of calm sophistication. Some of the shops and street-corner enterprises have a wacky, let's-give-it-a-go quality and are unselfconsciously using artifacts borrowed from any moment between the eighteenth and twenty-first centuries. It is the luscious impurity of the city's main product, port wine, that seems to characterize its attitude to life and architecture.

As the roads weave around and through the built city, they cross the river on two levels at the same moment. Is this indecision, a wonderful nonchalance, or a healthy overprovision? Just the same type of decision as the airport-extenders are making a hundred years later.

Other places have a response to invention that is more definite, and we can study them as agents of future cities. What would the little string of towns that run along the valley of the River Wupper in Westphalia have become without the insertion in 1928 of the aerial railway? It is tall and clanky and undeniably industrial in its iconography. It is gawky in the way it negotiates the bends in the river, over which it sits for much of its several kilometers' length. Just occasionally, it even dives in and out of a building. The cab hangs from the steel structure. Since that time the towns have coagulated into a city called Wuppertal. I like to think that this weird megastructure has given it a spirit beyond local politics. In the same way that the conglomeration of bridges in Newcastle-upon-Tyne, or the threading of highways over the edges of the river both in Brisbane and (again) Oporto give a clue to the possibilities of the two-string route-way and, ultimately, the three-dimensional city. Bridges and overhangs remind us of the hidden potential of structures, as do sports stadiums. They exist as fragments of the really intense and compounded city structure, but they can exist in relative isolation. I realized this when, on a languid summer evening after traveling through many miles of well-treed, languid countryside, a giant seating dish suddenly rose up out of the verdure. It was the shock announcement of the presence of a busy campus in Clemson, South Carolina. In the same vein, the dangling of sewage pipes and cables below many great bridges is a reminder that the guts of the city can be continued through space. **Plug-in City** was subconsciously the product of such phenomena even more than it was a concise statement about malleable form.

Opposite: **PLUG-IN CITY, AXONOMETRIC (Peter Cook, 1964)**
The megastructure clothed in undulating swathes of capsules with hovercraft as "buildings," inflatable skins and constant exchange of parts—an urbanism living on dynamic.

The insertion of a great sewer, Calcutta.

Systems invade the countryside.

The Shibuya section of Tokyo, a city of exploding surfaces.

Invention—Down to the Smallest Detail

Insidiously, the contemporary city is dependent upon unseen devices lurking just below the pavement, hidden inside the walls, or tucked in somewhere along a shaft or a tube; our mobilized existence is ever more dependent upon microchips. Ever more "unseen" and immensely effective. So at both scales we increase our fetishist delight in the outcrops that *can* be seen and touched. In Japan, the tanks on the tops of multistory buildings are draped with "quasi-architecture" that announces the company name or some vibrant symbol; these tanks effectively destroy the borderline between what is and what is not legitimate built form. Standard equipment, such as attached air-conditioning boxes, is less glamorous but becomes sufficiently universal for us to accept as building elements. In such a place our polite and regulated assumptions of legitimacy, generic types, substance, or completeness are challenged. On reflection, such assumptions were surely inherited from Classical thinking—a notion that every known element should have its place in the hierarchy. So we have also to look at Japanese psychology, where a certain devil-may-care attitude has infiltrated the ordered view of the world and where all the wires, pipes, boxes, and devices might eventually be developed into a rationale or even a cohesive aesthetic.

We might at this point ask a parallel question: is the proposition that cities be made up of complete buildings or complete city blocks necessary or appropriate? Sure, it makes sense to the street cleaners, the fire brigade, and the land lawyers, but it may not be in the best interests of the development of an architecture of response or of responsibility. It coagulates form and process in a series of "boxed" offerings that these late-twentieth-century phenomena seem to be able to do without.

Yet a walk along a city street will reveal clues of elastic systems, and as we glance at them we can surely indulge in a certain mental alchemy: we can surmise the lines of force from nighttime photographs of light trails, from lines of fire hydrants, from trains of consistent manholes. Large cities have hidden rivers: in London the Fleet and the Westbourne give their name to well-known streets but also, somewhere below, they run gurgling down to the Thames. So the classic film *The Third Man* alerted the mid-twentieth century to the significance of the Viennese sewers. More recently, the laying of cable television networks and the infestation of almost every workplace with multiplying sheaves of cabling suggest that formal or rectilinear proximity is no longer the issue. All these elements—water, gas, signals—zap through any artery that encourages them. And what of smart glass? Or of flat loudspeakers or flat imaging? The spread of forces onto and immediately across surfaces: why should it surprise us? For we exist among climatic conditions that respect few boundaries and radio waves that respect even fewer.

We can deliberately choose to misinterpret, imagining the manholes to be portals to immense and marvelous caves; the light trails to be energy waves of some wonderful, dynamic city structure; the potential of any surface to be that of any induced image, induced energy, induced climate—or just about anything imaginable. Put these all together and you have a vocabulary of architecture that is energy-based but also potentially spatial.

But what has been the status of these elements thus far? The fire hydrants and manholes followed the logic of the streets (as have many other facilities, including underground railways), but the potential of services to twist and leap and jump is also on offer. Smart glass tends to be trapped in window frames, and loudspeakers tend to be placed at thumpy points of significance. Early installations of electric lights followed the mannerisms of lanterns. Was there a certain instinct for tradition instilled in these provisions? "Let's have new facilities but not new icons"? More recently, we have begun to absorb views of the world manipulated by the camera and the computer to represent reality, and the trickery is accepted as a part of life. Encouraged, enjoyed, played with, dabbled with: many of us *prefer* the re-created image to that of the tarnished or commonplace object. Photo-derived techniques have entered the architectural territory and, through these electronic means, lead directly into a tantalizing world, that of virtual reality. At the time I was making my drawing **Room of 1000 Delights** I was only dimly aware that we could simulate the notion of endless space and the sensation of skimming across it—to be enjoyed as the experience of a room rather than a spacecraft. Yet in the time since the drawing was made, the idea has become commonplace.

In combining all of these wonderlands we must not merely repeat the cautious instincts that went before. The very audacity of making an architecture from what is not there, combined with the retreat and miniaturization of apparatus, will, I hope, redefine the rules. Relativity and systematization could retreat. More likely is the opportunity to make a combined architecture of what is there and what is not there—*together*.

ROOM OF 1000 DELIGHTS
(Peter Cook, 1970)

The Food Truck Syndrome and the Theater

Somewhere at the back of the city the wily entrepreneur sniffs the air, decides that there's a market, and sends out the happy truck. It parks on the corner and the local workforce heads out there, discovering not only sandwiches, drinks, and potato chips but endless other goodies. Experimental architects of the 1960s planted bubbles and capsules onto random patches of solid city blocks, and in the early 1990s the notion of the "parasite" structure was a standard conversation in architecture schools. Those kiosks in Tel Aviv or Berlin, or the endless scattering of drinks-and-candy shops in Buenos Aires are quizzical objects, but altogether traditional in both their informality and assertiveness. The truck and the bubble are far more fly-by-night. In a really vital city we should regard them as anything but special and suggest that the built form of a city is just a basic ground upon which almost anything may impinge.

A legitimate tradition exists on the theater stage, where illusion, concealment, decoy, and exchange make for the experience of place around the theatrical action. Even the eighteenth-century landscapists borrowed from such devices. It could also be argued that the dividing line between theatricality and mannerist facade-making all but disappeared. Yet I wish to beam the spotlight on the essentially *operational* devices of the theater: the gadgets and the fast-change apparatus, the puff of smoke and the appearance of the wizard. The methods involved accelerated and developed in the television studio—interestingly, in the same period that also saw the widespread development of assembly-line production and robotics in the factory. A culture in which a room, a zone, or an operation did not need to be locked together. They could emerge, split, reconfigure, exchange, or cease to exist. Every building an encampment? Every action a free-spirited act? If the theory of building began to borrow from this interplay rather reluctantly in the 1960s, '70s, and '80s, the response of the city conglomerate seems to have been even more sluggish. Tapping into the infrastructure still seems to be a messy, muddy business. Buildings are exchanged as a last resort—and expensively. The flexibility that is acceptable for an airport remains suspect in the city square. However friendly and familiar the forklift truck might be, it is consigned to the nether regions of our civilized world, like a hairy servant in a nineteenth-century drama. Strange that the elevator was easily accepted in polite society but devices with a parallel service for our current needs are kept from view. The street and the sidewalk and the entrapped conduits below are held in a time warp of function and expression.

Blackpool, a classic ice-cream van, 1930s or 1940s design. The ideal "capsule."

Bournemouth, cliff lift, early-twentieth-century design. Prototype moving building regularly observed by Peter Cook as a fledgling architecture student, two blocks away.

Climbing machine.

Lifting machine.

Feeding machine.

No wonder that we all got excited about robots in the 1960s. Not just the humanoid "walkabout" robots, but the whole idea of robotics and servicing and the possibilities of gadgetry as a natural extension of the vocabulary of architecture. These strange gizmos were able to monitor temperature, sound, and vibration, able to respond to distantly issued signals. But they were responding through something more than just the scale of a little, twitching gadget—the scale of whole chunks of building. Naturally, this was a questionable new experience for those who were most comfortable with the status of architecture as a stable, inert rock only one step from nature. It was a challenging new experience for those who were already suspicious that architecture was taking a backseat in the real world of action. Not totally new, however, as a trajectory, for the Victorians had managed to take on board all those metallic pipes and tubes and brackets and pulleys dragged from ships, harbors, and factory floors and onto the flanks of discreet villas. Sometimes they were wrought into brilliant greenhouses or turbine rooms, but it still seemed that "correct" architecture was eager to shy away again from all this show of apparatus. Many Modernist buildings delighted in presenting to the world only stark forms and smooth flanks (gadgetry was hidden away, for it distracted the eye). Inventions and legitimized gadgetry had to creep slowly back through the enthusiasm offered by a later mannerism, namely, high-tech architecture.

No wonder I remain excited by the myriad of interrelated systems by which we access goods in a warehouse, transport ourselves during a busy day, buy insurance, keep working while on the move, run an office from a small device carried in the palm of the hand. Our Archigram work was dedicated to the *extension* of the vocabulary of architecture. I believed then (and still do) that the devices we offer remain too comfortably based on the premise of keeping out of the weather and offering an agreeable space. We are in the *experience* business. We are there to offer more—more options, more experiences, more alternatives. We can make "Dreams Come True" (the title of one of Michael Webb's most evocative projects from the early 1970s) in a much more attainable way than he could ever have imagined at the time. A similarly relaxed approach is needed in the comprehension of the parts of architecture as with the parts of day-to-day electronics.

Insertions into the City

The Tongue was a naughty thing to lay down on the quiet street below the ancient hill in Graz. As the "lid" of a gallery, it was to contain a special world of consciously assembled artworks, but in itself it deliberately challenged the ability of the street to contemplate the new. Its "eyes" were to be augmented by small electrical devices that echoed the events going on within. The relationship of the Tongue to the street surface indulged in a non-chalant but cheeky positioning of the colored surface as *almost*—but never quite—a civic offering, so that you could walk on it, lie on it, peer into it, but never be quite sure whether it was street or building. Its progeny, **the Kunsthaus**, continues the same challenge, and as we hone the relationship between substance, surface, skin, electronics, hints, electrics, shadows, and anything else—both tangible and nearly intangible—we move toward a fusion of the latent and the induced.

The Buenos Aires art museum project that I now call **the Claws** is more overt. It sum-marizes many issues around the business of invention, implicitly uses a mixture of them discussed above, and at the same time suggests itself as a model for a more developed and integrated version of the "sheds" that exist around the edges of our cities.

The claws themselves are the antennae of the main building: they are the extension of its lines of force, and from these claws extend further antennae. Not that the term *main building* should rest too comfortably, either. True, it is the largest mass. True, it houses the most permanently located galleries, but more important, it is the shed or "depot" from which the rest of the art park is serviced. It sits without too much articulation: a cheap skin building but with plenty of opportunity for the more set-piece art to be viewed from a variety of positions. Its stairs and platforms are fairly busy, its profile fairly nonchalant. But then there is the park component.

At the farthest end of the park, there are the remains of some gardening by Roberto Burle Marx, one of the heroes of my student days (and one of the few who did not disap-point me as a person). I inserted some more trees and bushes, then prepared the ground between by inducing a variety of surfaces and some preferred lines of force, but only enough for the real action to grasp onto. The claws reach out, and with their family of tents, boards, gantries, prepared patches—and whatever else is brought in by the partici-pating artists—the main gallery takes shape. More is to come, for out of the bushes can pop various instantaneous or discrete or quizzical vignettes. And *all is not what it seems* in Marx's little wood at the end. The ground is not to be too flat, either: as if it were a par-ody of a piece of rural lowlands, there are gentle undulations and patches of irregularity (my own take on the Japanese game of ritualistic representation, perhaps?).

THE CLAWS PROJECT, BUENOS AIRES ART PARK
(Peter Cook, 1997)
The main gallery shed (right) is also a depot for the movable and tunable armatures, sheds, tents, decks, and lights that occupy the central apron area. In the trees and bushes (left), a remnant of the garden designed by Roberto Burle Marx, there can be further elements of apparatus waiting to "claw" the event-space.

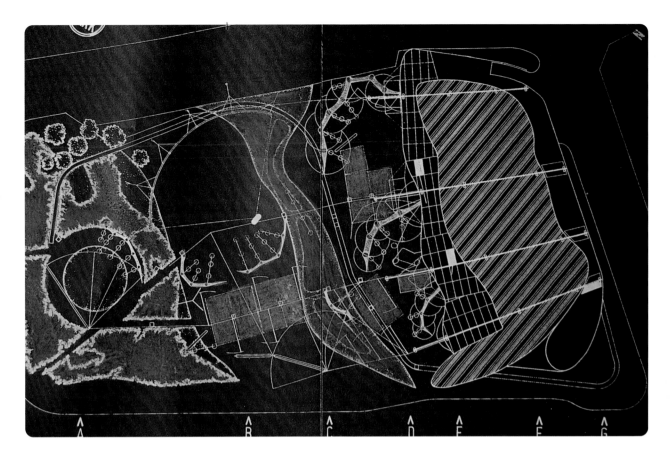

THE CLAWS PROJECT
Detail of serviced art-yard.

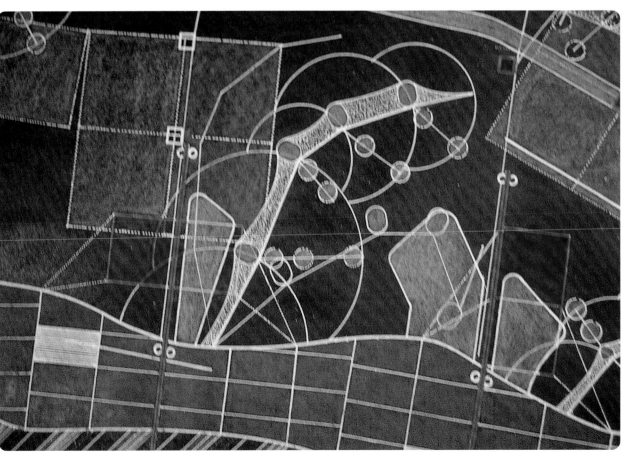

Essential to the philosophy of this building is the eagerness with which I anticipate the cybernetics of the *show* itself. In the **Monte Carlo Entertainments Center** (which predates the Claws by some twenty-seven years), the various options within the underground shed were to be manipulated by the visiting producer of each show. He or she could assemble the available robotry to be radical (or not) by positioning everything from toilets to neck microphones. Similarly, with the proposed audiovisual "buses" for the Graz Kunsthaus, mobile packages of robotic equipment were again to be positioned and manipulated by the artists themselves. This seeming avoidance of mandate as an architect is anything but. In a creative scenery one is an artist talking to other artists: surely they (if anyone) want to engage in the creation of the theater of the place. But in a way it is also a form of provocation, for many artists are irritated by the way in which architects of the 1980s and 1990s bullied them into playing a minor role within a great sculptural envelope. An edgy atmosphere emerged in a period in which several key artists wish to make environmental objects (effectively "architecture"), and this instinctively irritates architects. The invitation offered by the Claws and the Kunsthaus is to take up the story just where it gets interesting: to use the territory and the apparatus provided and for *somebody* to get in there and make the *place*.

To expect something like this to happen to your neighborhood food mart is as yet idealistic. Though in history, the value of the heroically cultural statement has often been recognized long afterward as its influence drifts slowly down via the theater of parody, imitation, and commercialism. The Buenos Aires patch is deliberately a mixture of intense and loose elements—interdependent but with a relaxed attitude toward the space between the large shed and the next large building (directly across a single wide street, as it happens). It is not a collection of bitsy buildings, nor is it a bland car lot, nor is it a piece of axial geometry. The shed is incomplete without the garden, and the garden is meaningless without the shed. What is hinted at here is a creative attitude toward the large patches between large buildings. What is suggested is an appropriation—and a joyous exposure—of devices, services, apparatus of all kinds. As they interact with each other, their task is to make a continuous form of **Instant City.** The old scheme of that name, devised at the end of the 1960s, needed mobility and shock as its generic ingredients. Now we have all those patches of space that sit nervously (and often tackily) between foursquare (and usually pastiched) chunks of architecture. The American block system and its parking-lot syndrome accept them a little more relaxedly than does the European tradition. Even the English looseness is a crevice-y looseness—odd things lurking, hidden behind, tucked in, but no, no, not in great patches. Hence this mixture of bewilderment and the cultural advantage that we might have if we only knew how to use it.

As the available devices are observed and then mixed and remixed there is always that old pressure of calm discrimination that almost seems to act as a limiting factor. As I swing along the newly created pathway at Heathrow Airport and count up the features, I am a mental sponge. Yet as I sit plotting the pathways and incidents of **Graz** or **Pinto** a day or two afterward, I proceed hierarchically: the main lines first, the main functional patches next, the systems and icons next, *and then* the devices. Such irony, such stubbornness. Cedric Price is, as ever, the seer in this situation: it was he who coined the term *scrambled egg* for the urban condition. Justice to the act of scrambling implies a continuous mental activity.

Sitting in that part of London just beneath the hill of Hampstead, I have been able to play with a useful patch of ground in our neighborhood that lies tantalizingly against the part of the hill that contains Europe's highest concentration of psychoanalysts. It still has some open land that occurs through the intersection of three railways. It is inner suburbia—patchy and eccentric, accustomed to the sound of professional pianists and the rantings of speculative intellectuals. Tantalizingly close and tantalizingly redolent of all kinds of antennae (both physical and contextual). The **Dampstead** project, of 1994, strode across the territory in a series of giant feet that were shod on one side by induced vegetation and on the other side by tough, rational slabs of wall. It carried most of its infrastructure with it. In the context of this chapter, it chose to skip over the laid ground and only posit its own energies at each end of the journey. The next project for the site was, however, much more of an essay about built town.

The **Finchley Road** scheme took off from the proposition that there could be a series of serviced walls, or "wafts," that swirled along and around the railway tracks. They could also form wraps around odd patches of site, more or less in the manner of normal walls. They would contain a mix of uses particularly suited to such a part of London (don't forget that I had been a local for many years). Creative cynicism was the clue. Many shrinks. Many musicians. Many lawyers or accountants, some architects, some small-scale creative businesses. Some that played on the charm and money of Hampstead but needed good communications. A place that can be thick with dance schools and health clubs such as would be found in the lower west side of New York or the closer shores of Brooklyn. Here they would need a relaxed but commodious system of well-serviced barns that could be carved away and riddled with "specials conditions" that could come and go. More like studios than anything else but with plenty of outlets and supply lines.

This became a clue for the key feature: a series of twisting orange snakes, which have an immediate impact. They could never be lost or ignored and they had to have a presence far beyond anything else that was likely to be inserted. Instinctively they come from an extremely respectable parentage, namely, the Richards Medical Research Building by Louis Kahn, which dates from 1957. The great shafts that serve the foursquare blocks had a dramatic impact upon my generation of architects, finally asserting the legitimacy of service and facility, albeit with a calmness that the Finchley Road project would not enjoy. From then on, it can be seen that the sinews of many and varied supplies can be threaded together like a giant piece of cabling, but with the cables having a wide range of benefits and physiognomies. The orange thing shouts, "Come and get me," with its amazing range of fluids, smell of air, and specialist channels, which find expression in the grilles, outlets, plugs, and mats that inhabit its girth.

Working in these studios becomes an experience of straightforward action in a well-lined shed but also a constant invitation to more exotic experiences via the orange snake. It is as if the clever devices that are threaded around those airport extensions—out of sight but always on the case—are now formally introduced into the city space and yell out quite cheerfully as they enter it.

**DAMPSTEAD, FINCHLEY ROAD, LONDON, ELEVATION FROM THE SOUTH
(Peter Cook, 1995)**
A series of apartment blocks that step lightly down from Hampstead Village to the West Hampstead rail yards. The south face is planted, the north face is tight and insulated.

DAMPSTEAD, MODEL
The long views to the west are celebrated by the most open facade. Greenhouses continue the garden tradition of the area, and they sprout out independently of the main structure.

SNAKE SHEDS, FINCHLEY ROAD, LONDON
(Peter Cook, 1995–96)
The orange "snakes," a free-flowing service element, facilitate a mixed-use office and studio enterprise.

SNAKE SHEDS, INTERIOR

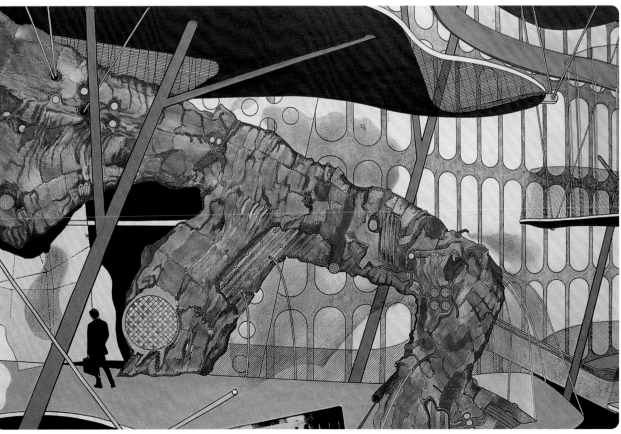

The City as a Lively Hedge

Inventing a total piece of town is a much more scary experience, especially when you are also guessing the future. Who might they be and what *more* can we offer them? If Finchley Road was a case of daily observation, creative cynicism about one's neighbors, and then a hefty lob of cheeky ideas in their direction, the project for **Pinto** has quite different overtones.

It is in a flat, open, hardly developed landscape. It is close to Madrid—a strong, hard, proud city. You arrive at it along a freeway, past the Motel los Angeles and turn right at the Pinto MacDonald's, a stucco neoclassic pavilion (yes, you really could be *anywhere* in the Western world). It adjoins a recently developed township where the blue-collar heritage is being subtly manipulated toward a white-collar ethos. Yet in other ways it might respond to the same aspirations as those of suburban London. The rather straight and closed manner of Madrid's housing blocks are not inspiring, but the recent emancipation of the Spanish worker and his family is exciting as a challenge not to be *too* polite. Soon, they too will need those dance studios and psychoanalysts.

With Salvador Arroyo and Eva Hurtado as my codesigners and guides, I started to invent a world where the mannerisms and hang-ups of the old cities can be ignored. Where "workplace" as such is an anachronism. Where "institution" or "club" or "retail outlet" are limited definitions, where "hangout" and "lookout" are useful reminders of what we like to do in a good city, where "street corner" or "plaza" might have sufficed in the past but must be replaced by something better and possibly more subtle.

A three-kilometer strip of new city must be made, and behind it (away from the existing town of Pinto) is proposed a network of partially occupied countryside—an update of the atmosphere of orchards, market gardens, golf courses, and parks that have become eroded elsewhere. Within this "garden" zone there are occasional outcrops with housing resting on them. The flat, arid plateau can be infected with a planted but also inhabited carpet that perhaps harks back to the Northern Europe of the 1920s or 1930s—a time of social and territorial experiment. Yet it is in the strip itself that one has the clearest vision of a new type of city, one where the increasingly usable edges of people's timetables will be responded to by a more malleable architecture and enclosure. Aided by devices and facilities, which offer possibilities of openly enjoying a condition that is allowed to be simultaneously *work* and *play*.

The Pinto strip runs along the top of a series of small, man-made hills that fold relaxedly in and out of the built state. In other words, the lower parts of the strip are made up of heaped earth, as well as roads and parking structures. Dashing along the top and bottom

STAEDELSCHULE CANTEEN, FRANKFURT
(Peter Cook and Christine Hawley, 1990–93)

STAEDELSCHULE CANTEEN, FRANKFURT

of the hill are paths and boardwalks—or perhaps they might be called board-runs. I fully expect them to be the province of joggers and cyclists who might even become an updated version of the show-offs of Los Angeles's Muscle Beach, especially against the backdrop of so many offices-as-lounges, eateries, and places in which to shelter from the sun. The boardwalks cling to the north side of the hills. Sometimes they zigzag up the hills and even zig right up the side of the largest hotels and other major structures. These have gardens, tennis courts, bowling greens, and aviaries on their roofs. They have a series of pools jumping down beneath them and into the hill. Most of these buildings are active "racks" that can absorb office work, selling work, display work, educational work, half work, no work, residency, or mixed living-and-doing. Snakes slightly more circumspect than those at Finchley Road can rise up from within the hill to bring the major supplies and palliatives. Little wiry slivers can creep up through the layers of louvers and smart glass that erratically sheathe the racks.

The most intense part of this hilltop is a form of acropolis in which a series of curved strips traps the necessary breezes. There the boardwalk becomes a slightly formalized, semicircular "parade," and the buildings can be read as part of an intentional "sandwich" system. It consists of: *hard base* (the car parking and health clubs within the hill), *soft undercroft* at boardwalk level (to take kiosks, bars, huts, buskers, and anything else of a random presence), *hard four-floor structure* (office racks), and *soft roof*, where games and planting can be laid on all the roofs-as-parks.

All around there are snippets of institution, but at a very local scale: taps, switches, pads, dedicated gratings, sockets . . . and quickly up the scale to kiosks, fountains, icon-robots, tents, belvederes—all woven into an ongoing fabric. But not a street to be seen. Every potential "block" is melted before it really congeals. The vertical surfaces of screens and absorbers of wind, heat, or imagery become the most noticeable iconography. The techniques of the airport and the harbor, the theater and the factory are here to be developed, and if it is sometimes all too busy, you pull in from a wide selection of veils and architectonic parasols.

I now realize that (with Christine Hawley) I once built a little piece of Pinto (though it was in Frankfurt). Our canteen for the Staedelschule is light casual and is folded into the surrounding structure. Whether it is really a piece of building at all is ambiguous because it flaps open in the warm weather and grins at you and then flaps shut again and remains looking as if it might take off any minute.

Surely cities are itching to be like this?

PINTO TOWN EXTENSION, MASTER PLAN
(Peter Cook, Salvador Perez-Arroyo, Eva
Hurtado, as of March 2001)
A satellite town to Madrid will be extended
to house over 15,000 people and incorporate
hotels, a college, high-tech offices, sales
centers, a hospital, and a golf course. The
totally flat site is to be animated by moving
earth and creating an artificial "sierra" at
the head of which is a tight cluster of flowing hotels and agencies.

PINTO TOWN EXTENSION, DETAIL
Left center: Club building.
Right center: Kiosks on boardwalk.

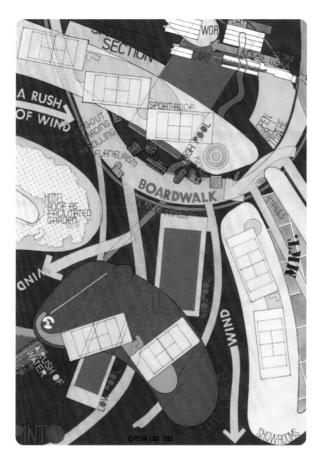

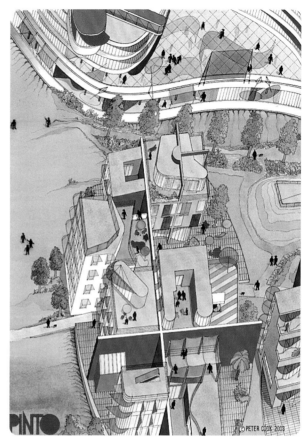

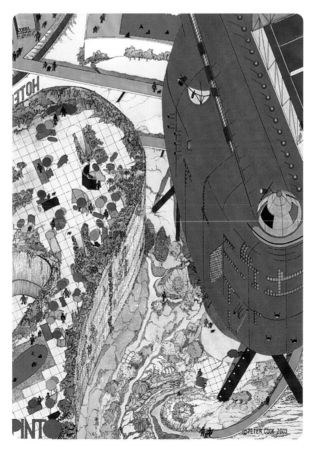

THE CITY OF GARDENS

In Los Angeles, the perfect insertion of high architecture
into nature is found in the Charles and Ray Eames
House, 1949.

Palm House at Kew, London (James Turner, 1851).

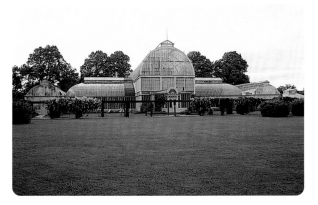

Palm House, Gothenburg.

Palm House, Kyoto.

Inside-Outside Revisited

No walls: great! The garden coming right in: great! A continuum from the den to the farthest tree: great!

In one move, the unlikely trio of Mies van der Rohe, Richard Neutra, and Frank Lloyd Wright—not to mention Marcel Breuer and Rudolf Schindler—managed to combine three romantic ideals from differenttwo very epochs in a simple and reproducible formula. The home and the restaurant are two of the most relaxing environments for most of us, and both reach this state without strict categorization of space. Even the easily embarrassed English have finally taken to the idea of the open-air café and bring themselves to admit that their private indulgence can be a piece of the general landscape. For Modernist architects, though, the whole business of the wall-less wall was the consequence of plate-glass technology and the triumph of "look-no-hands!" engineering. The consequence of free planning. The consequence of that repeated Modernist image: the view through the piloti and the gentle rolling-through of the ground.

The encompassment of the garden was played with far earlier, especially in those damp islands of Japan and Britain, where picturesque vegetable growth happens almost automatically. Bringing the most varied combinations of plants into the house and then (if you had the space) making the house itself reach out around those plants was a game of gardening and architecture played interactively. The Victorians, as they traveled, became ambitious for something more: these homegrown greens were not enough. How could they bring exotica of the Orient or the desert into their domain?

Inventive engineers and technologists of the day supplied the answer. Iron and glass contrivances erupted all around the gardens of Europe, sometimes with wonderful formal power. Kibble Palace in Glasgow or the Palm House at Kew are forerunners of the inflatable shapes of the 1960s or the computer-generated surfaces of the 1990s. The Orangery at Chatsworth is a forerunner of the glass slivers that Bruno Taut in the 1920s or Emilio Ambasz in the 1980s might have threaded over the landscape. They introduced the idea of the internal but cosseted garden, and already the idea of outside-existing-inside was under way. Spreading to every bourgeois conservatory, it related well to the German notion of the winter garden and an English activity that extended our coyness toward animals in the direction of tomatoes or sunflowers.

The notion that "all that you can see is one continuum" runs further back, however. Perhaps to the feudal hierarchies, perhaps to the lookout tower of the castle where the contemplated world was not just a notion of control but of interrelatedness of all types of phenomena: of trees and buildings, of language and habits, of scattered pieces of contrivance (walls, gates, ditches, tracks, clearings, forges, paddocks). There was no dividing line between these contrivances and natural growths. Political stability and the partial democratization of power led inevitably to a stylization of these assumptions.

For those with power, money, and influence, the absorption of formal arrangements coming from Classical principles and not a little from the mannerisms of the theater soon began to impose rituals of design upon that same contemplated world. Furthermore, this could be exaggerated as a picturesque progression. With immense detail and control of

Castle Drogo gardens, Devonshire. (Lutyens)

Late Victorian garden, Sheffield.

the interior of the salons and the principal bedrooms of great houses, the picture through the window could be one of hard focus melted back to soft focus. Considerable detail and control (if possible with articulated wings of the building, or at least with gazebos) on the terraces. A conscious breakaway of the gardens beyond: still mannered and controlled. Then another conscious breakaway to the park that was implicitly part of the whole composition but with the additional mannerisms that emerge through vegetation. Perhaps then—and only then in the scheme of things—would a distant mountain, hill, or patch of sea be allowed to remind us of another, outer world.

The three ideals came together remarkably easily—democratized and remarkably light. At the scale of the homestead you hardly needed a major piece of engineering to open up a whole wall, nor did you need to create a separate conservatory if you chose your plants well, pumped in enough energy, fitted sophisticated glazing—or happened to live in Palm Springs anyway. And though you were not the baron of all you could see, the very polyphony of growths, artifacts, appliances, surfaces, gadgets, and domestic toys—from the farthest cactus via the hairiest fern through the laziest hammock to the cutest Jacuzzi—acted as such a magical continuum that it hardly mattered. Perhaps it was even some primeval instinct that reminded us that any building is but a temporary interruption in the ultimate rolling and groaning and metamorphosis of the ground; and that those damned weeds will get back again some time, so why not learn to love them?

The notion that the edge line of the building is no heroic moment contains a certain paradox, for it seems at first a modest surrendering of the architect's power. Let it all hang out, let it slip—who cares? Alternatively, it represents a moment of confidence at which architecture can be both totally relaxed and in control of the issue of "object," "boundary," "room," "domain," and "place." Inside can be outside, too. And vice versa. Even in England it was worth the occasional shiver.

For my own work, the inside-outside model has always been there as an objective—almost there as a right. The outside was to be accessible and graspable, like fresh orange juice. Like the presence of a tree immediately outside. (The two short periods in which I have lived away from a proximate tree have been hauntingly miserable.) It has fitted well with an extended fascination with the idea of the soft boundary and the sense of "it's there—it's not there" and it has fitted well with the attractions of the continuous grain of found and invented parts, irrespective of whether they are strictly "architecture" or not.

The London Garden Wall and "Tree Houses"

Unfortunately for the American observer, the English have a predilection for hiding and therefore find themselves attracted to the idea of the walled garden—in many ways an opposite objective from the last proposition. If the wall implies fear, uncertainty, assertion before the implicit questioning of rights or mandates, it is also the product of our wish for the primacy of the built form: we grab and then we make. Then we release some space and a very controlled remnant of nature is allowed to creep up again. But the nature itself can be the controlling factor: certain pieces of topiary are not only an exercise in quaintness—all those trimmed birds and animals—but also a reinstatement of man's control over nature. In extreme cases, the trimmed hedge can be as comely and seem as solid as any castle wall. Indeed, Edwin Lutyens's Castle Drogo in Devon presents us with a set of architectonic spaces and articulated vistas that have no need for masonry, so disciplined is the hedgery. If we add to this the Tuscan importation of the pergola, we have enough ingredients for a whole system of architecture.

Yet the essence of such an architecture is not just a question of balancing these parts together, for paradoxically the critical ingredient is the one that has so far been the suppliant: the vegetation itself. By its diffusion and its lack of respect for the predictability of normal pieces of construction, it can become both a threat and a promise of something far more exotic. There is something risky and even spooky about designing with vegetation, especially when it is playing back and forth with the formally built. It is a Romantic game, but one in which the essential life force of the wispy tentacles that soon start to spread is capable of overwhelming the well-mannered armatures of fabric or the thickset hedges. It has its own speeds of growth and cycles of coloration and decay. It is essentially dynamic and not completely predictable. Yet it can be aided and abetted by the stoicism of the built form that it might creep along.

In the view across the gardens of inner suburban houses, there are series of nuances that are somehow built up by various *layerings* of growth. They seem to follow the boundaries of the gardens and the rhythm of open patches rather reluctantly, and thus they soon confound the observer. At the right time of the year the growths are totally dominant and the houses peek out here and there from within. Perhaps it is all to do with the craving for the countryside; perhaps it is an admission of the paucity of character in the buildings themselves—the camouflage eagerly awaited as early spring begins. Character and place are established by trees, by patches of similar texture, by shadows, by shimmers and fading patches, by density imperceptibly giving way in a dissolve.

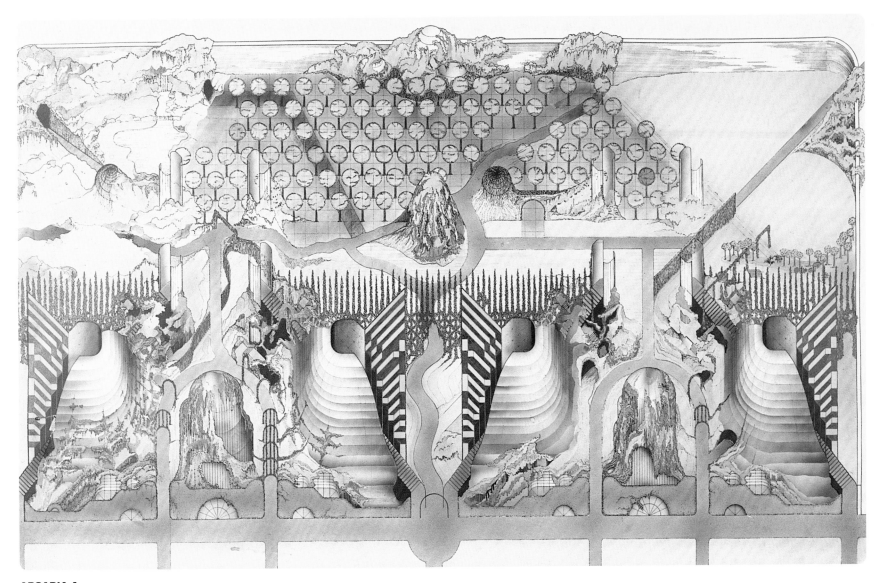

ARCADIA A

Orangery to Schloss Karlsruhe, Karlsruhe.

Detail of garden-armatures, Schwetzingen.

Detail of garden-armatures, Schwetzingen.

Containment, Rousham, Oxfordshire. (William Kent)

Shigakuin gardens, Kyoto.

Now try to reinterpret that in built terms. An architecture of seasonal change? Of shimmer and fade? Of imperceptible dissolve? Even the most Gothic or the most expressionist moments fall far short of these modest suburban gardens.

In a project of the 1980s I found myself delving into the garden for sustenance as well as the conscious discovery of points where the one (architecture) could be merged with the other (planting). **Arcadia A** was nonetheless quite urban. No escape to the country here, integration giving no pretense that the scheme was not a building. No games with distance. The whole thing in a box, the rear part walled. Unashamedly borrowing from the Cook-Hawley **Via Appia House** and interpreting it as an apartment block, repeating it and its "grotto" area as the first stage in a dissolve. The garden proper has a Romantic end and a bland end and contains an orchard and a lawn. These standard components are then teased by a few more quizzical objects that are *both* vegetation and enclosure. One such sits on the wall, another pops up out of the ground. The dense hedge on the street side is clearly inhabited, perhaps nostalgically by the semicircular "studio" windows. Indeed, there is plenty of nostalgia here for the Via Appia project itself, which remained for a long time full of source material—we had talked so many ideas into what had, after all, been a minor competition item. The instinctive feel of the place somewhere in the inner London territories of Belsize Park, Holland Park, or Bedford Park—and by no accident the whole issue of park and its studied artificiality is closely linked to that of the escape out of architecture into vegetation. A vegetation that is, in the end, mannered and controlled. There are the memories of so many childhood gardens and damp, creepy patches. The memories of damp but variegated days. And surely watercolor is the only appropriate coloring medium for any drawing of such compositions.

In later projects in the Arcadia series, the idea of the tree as a prototypical house would crop up again and again. Standing under, or rather within, a large willow is a childhood delight: enclosure with filtered light. Plant and building as one. What could be better? Now build it, plant it, could it not really be a house? Replace the trunk by a similarly organic but *serviced element*? Make some additional conditions of skin and screening?

Out of the Winter Garden

The other route is to take off where the conservatories and winter gardens left off. It is back to the apparatus of trellis, pergola, orangery, terrace, conservatory. Normally considered appendages, they can, if we want, serve as generic maneuvers. The nineteenth-century construction that sits onto the orangery wall at the castle of Karlsruhe is not glazed. Perhaps it was at one time. I certainly don't want to know, because onto its framework the strands and branches are wrapped throughout the winter and in its web there come the growths of the summer. And by the way, the backdrop of "inhabited" wall, with a narrow restaurant sitting within, has the necessary quality of minimum, even supportive architectural activity, thus throwing the emphasis back out and under the large-scale trellis. This particular case has a certain rhetoric, since it lies at the core of the great geometric construct of Park and City that forms Karlsruhe with the enclosure being of sufficient size to lift it out of the appendage category anyway.

Fifty kilometers north are the gardens of Schwetzingen, and it is here that I have been

KAWASAKI INFORMATION CITY, a.k.a. FRANKFURT GARDEN MUSEUM, elevation (left part).
(Peter Cook, 1986)
A project developed for both the Kawasaki competition and as a part of the "Real City" program for Frankfurt.

KAWASAKI INFORMATION CITY, a.k.a. FRANKFURT GARDEN MUSEUM, section.

KAWASAKI INFORMATION CITY, a.k.a. FRANKFURT GARDEN MUSEUM, elevation (right part).
The Kyoto gardens and their progression of small pavilions as a route system are here reinterpreted *vertically*.

repeatedly inspired by the arched trellising. Again, it works both in winter and summer. Unashamedly a device for marking and routing through territories of the park, it establishes just sufficient armature for the growing elements to act fairly predictably. In this sense, compared with the London gardens, it is not by any means disposed to mystery, though there is a place for this later: in a selected corner, the same trellising sets up an arcade that focuses into a controlled vista and a delightful (and inevitably Romantic) vision of a mysterious bower . . . far away. Of course, the whole thing is a trompe l'oeil construct (it is painted onto the back wall of a form of camera obscura). This little vignette catches me up sharp. Being of a Modernist upbringing, I can claim so far to have kept the argument for Romance through vegetation as a clean game. Even if you don't always know quite what you are looking at, you are certainly looking at a *something*. Even if you don't quite know where (or when) one condition turns into another, it *does* turn and it i*s* there. The tree as a house is still some sort of *replacement*. But those eighteenth-century Italian garden designers in Schwetzingen were up to something else: an equivalent of today's cyberspace made with paint and light-angles.

The Garden as Protocity

Most good architecture has to create a séance. Even the most contextually conscious response has to concentrate at some point upon the aura of the newly created place. Memories, symbols, tricks, emphases, deliberate suppressions—they are all there. Once stated, they relax back into time and a decade later may seem even quaint, the séance having already become just a ghostly whiff. Somehow the garden, because of its seasonal cycle and its slow maturity, can never have the same degree of response. Neither can it have the same drop-off.

The frustration of the intangible becomes its temptation. Apart from the most boneheaded municipal gardeners who plant patches of red or yellow flowers bounded by a strict geometric figure, the husbandry of the garden is much more akin to the vagaries of the city outside than to the constructed pavilion. Both are buffeted by weather and unpredictable interlopers; both grow almost imperceptibly. Visually, too, they share the condition of infinite interpretation or misinterpretation: vistas are endless, detail is endless.

Despite one's attachment to the policy of design as a linked chain—that whole Modernist belief that the same criteria make a good spoon, a good kitchen, a good hospital, a good suburb, and a good road system—there are places where such an edict begins to look foolish, particularly under a trailing vine or on the edge of a pool. In the garden, there is only the boundary of imagination set by the fence, but little boundary of influence. In Chapter 3 some of the motives of the Japanese, English, and German traditions were discussed. Already in the twenty-first century, the maker of a garden can call upon any mixture of aesthetic traditions and a similar mixture of chemical and technological aids to cheat the limitations of local climate. The battle of wills starts to come closer to the tradition of building: the creation of the artificial in the face of the natural. The battle of conscience is rarely heard: the wish to control against the delight in the imperfect.

If our observation of cities is enjoyed through the accumulation of major and minor elements together, we must reassess our view of things interstitial: those brushed-aside patches of infill, add-ons, peek-throughs, light relief. Not just the inevitable plea of the English picturesque-merchant. Even Washington, Ankara, or Brasilia must have engagingly frayed edges. Back in the garden, almost everything is interstitial: the bug, the worm, and certainly the mole have their role and there is interference at every turn. It becomes possible to create a long hierarchy of parts: from terrace through path, grassy bank, small planted patch to thinned-out leaves. We can all play city-maker. With or without the Japanese tradition of symbols or the Classical language of mannered references, we can literally "potter about," making conscious marks in space that are wide open to delightful misinterpretation by natural forces.

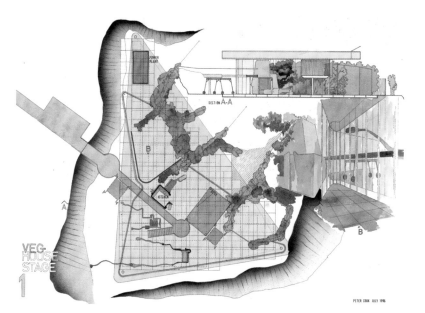

**VEG. HOUSE, Stage 1, plan and vignette.
(Peter Cook, 1996/2001)**

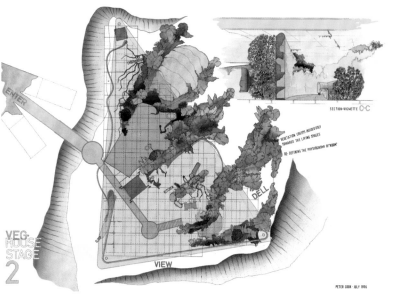

VEG. HOUSE, Stage 2, plan and vignette.

VEG. HOUSE, Stage 3, plan and vignette.

VEG. HOUSE, Stage 4, plan and vignette.

VEG. HOUSE, Stage 5, plan and vignette.

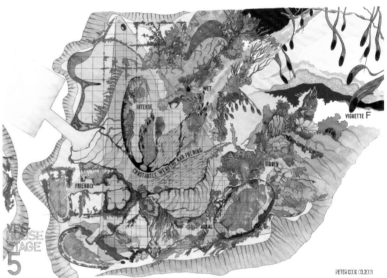

VEG. HOUSE, Stage 6, plan and vignette.

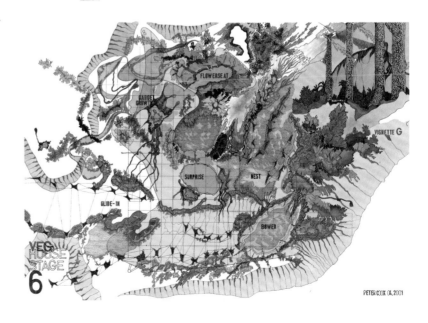

An Architecture That Celebrates Vegetation

The **Veg. House** sits on a shelf of hillside overlooking a river. A triangular table is established, held on the three corners. The table is a waffle of cover and servicing space. You approach on one of the longer sides. The space is tall enough for two floor heights, if needed. A power core is established near one corner. That's it. Very straightforward.

On closer observation, nearby vegetation is waiting to be invited into the triangulated space. There are some modest strings of trainer wires on offer within. Inevitably, the one will follow the other. The scheme is described in six phases. At the first, some fairly placid infilling is made. The double height is exploited by platforms. A sensible glazed skin wraps around the triangular shape. A trickle of planting moves along the trainers.

The second phase begins to welcome much more infiltration of vegetation. It also begins the process of weaving *spaces* out of that vegetation. The arrangement of "rooms" has shifted. The skin begins to deflect. Odd bedfellows such as kitchen appliances and bushes are encouraged to mix together. We realize that there is no such thing here as "house" or "garden." Nor necessarily the notion of the house stretching into the garden or just welcoming the garden into itself—the house *is* the garden. The next stages seem to accelerate the process, so that sound devices, heating devices, no doubt—at any moment—virtual-reality devices join into the plantation. And this notion of *plantation* is the clue to the whole project. In the past we clung to our comfortable definitions—of primary and secondary elements, of substance and surface, of appliances, devices, services, appendages, the "natural," the "artificial." By implanting the most contrived and artificial (and quizzical) of contemporary gizmos into the most wayward and relaxed substances—the bushes and vines—one posits a free-origin web of sound, smell, and comfort.

Somehow—and it could very well be a psychologically explainable release—some of the old, romantic-sounding terminologies seem highly appropriate: the glade, the bower, the arbor. And there was the return to words drifting around the drawing. These had been consciously avoided since Archigram times.

Neither drawings (which jump staccatolike from phase to phase), nor a model, nor verbal description can summon up the necessary atmosphere. Tectonics seem to remain, however: the power plant (rhetorically?) becomes smaller and smaller each time and the enclosing skin becomes trickier and more seductive. As time takes over, the infestations multiply but remain benign.

They are nice juicy vines. Not creepy-crawlies.

An urbanism of a sort had to come out of all this. After a few months reflection, I set up a small piece of hillside as a proposition. Covered patches arrived (no longer just triangles, but a variety of fairly useful shapes). Paths wander around in a useful way. Also, on closer inspection, there is a gridded system of service outlet points. The patches encourage enclosure and plantation as before. As time goes by, the covers and the rest increase in density.

Something else is happening as well: the development of patches that surely cannot be inhabited or enclosed but are undeniably imploded. Some have definite linear structure, some seem just to slurp all over the place. I realized that just to repeat the formula of covered plantation and paths was falling into the old house-and-patch trap. If this is to be a **Veg. Village,** it must welcome the wayward infestation of all conditions of ground—some of the patches are, of course, useful hydroponic gardening. I have always enjoyed those lichen-infested limpid pools found in English and Japanese gardens either waiting for the floating beauty to drift in off a pre-Raphaelite painting or doing something more useful, such as jolting us into questioning the true nature of such things as "surface" or "layer" or "wet" or "dry."

The **Veg. City** has yet to emerge.

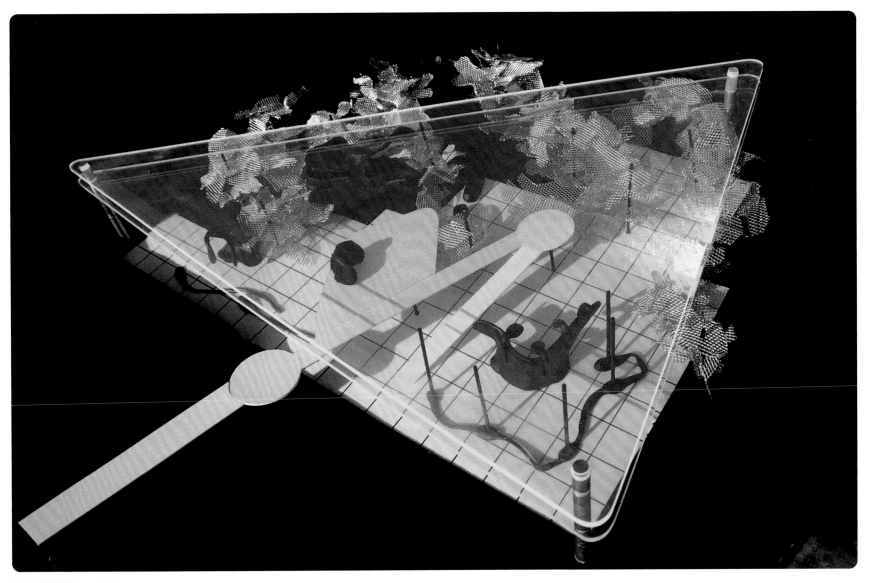

VEG. HOUSE, model.
Approximates the situation at Stage 2.

The Planted Object as Megastructure

At a certain moment I felt sufficiently comfortable with the notion of architectural plantation to make it the language of my return to the megastructure (some twelve years after **Plug-in City**) and applied the monster to two sites. One was in Frankfurt, where I was spending so much time that I could not just sit idly by without making a series of architectural suggestions (loosely bound together under the title **Real City**). I applied the vegetated scheme to a site that always seemed to tantalize: the Westhafen, which is a small finger trailing along the side of the river Main, near the main station. In the early stages I learned of a Japanese competition for the **Kawasaki Information City**, which had a very loose brief. From then on the two schemes became reversed versions of each other.

In Frankfurt the intention was to offer a vertical inhabited park as an alternative to the many new museums that were opening at that time, to bring people up out of the dusty town and into a constructed glade in which they would discover various small pavilions, each celebrating a cultural moment. The path from one to the next was part of a (mechanically assisted or ramped) slow climb allied to the variety of beckonings and deliberate pauses that I was about to borrow from Japanese gardens, even before the Kawasaki incentive. But the idea of Information City *did* affect the scheme, for it increasingly became a combination of overt elements—the pavilions and the paths—as well as covert suggestions of audio programs to be phased into patches of foliage, nighttime manifestations of lights and electronics, and some naughty technologized trees borrowed from the earlier projects of my friends Ron Herron and David Greene and able to broadcast sounds, affect climate, and create atmosphere.

Not just as cover for implanted goodies but as *architectural surface itself,* the vegetation was able to take on the role of enclosure at the lower levels. The megastructure could vary in intensity so growths, implantations, virtual copses, and then, at the tip of the harbor finger, a final coagulation of cabins to form a hotel. The vegetation of the earlier Lump and Mound projects was atmospheric; now it could be tectonic. One could delve into the compounded undergrowth of the restaurant-auditorium structure, one could peel away this undergrowth to reveal the hotel. The diagram of the building is a series of constructivist armatures.

The final form is undeniably hairy. Almost a barnacled wreck.

**VEG. VILLAGE, plan at Stage 1.
(Peter Cook, 1998)**

VEG. VILLAGE, plan at Stage 2.

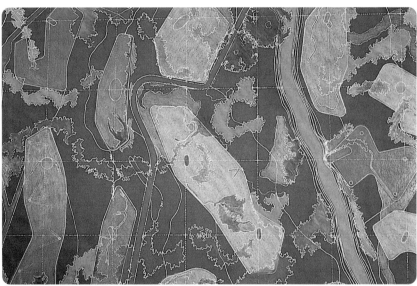

VEG. VILLAGE, plan at Stage 3.

7

THE CITY OF ICONS

City corner, Gothenburg.   **City corner, Gothenburg.**

Glances, Fixes, or Decoys?

For many years the split city of Berlin could glance at the needle-and-ball television tower in East Berlin. Locate it, blink in the sun, hear things radioed off it—do just about everything with it except *go there*. The politics of the situation led to some iconic tit-for-tat whereby Hugh Stubbins's scooped congress hall, Hans Scharoun's exuberant Philharmonie, and Mies van der Rohe's crisp elegance at the Nationalgalerie were signals sent back over the wall. In Paris, such signals are sent out by the Church of Saint Sulpice on Montmartre back to the Eiffel Tower and across to the towers of La Défense: such signaling is made on a skyline dimension. Whereas in the same city, those sent out by the main facade of l'Opéra toward its avenue, or the sharp corner of Jean Nouvel's Institut du Monde Arabe toward the embankment, though certainly powerful, remain part of a setting: a prepared street, a riverside. It helps to know just how far a signal needs to travel. How provocative the signal needs to be. Then, and only then, can a calculation be made about the necessary degree of revelation as you come closer and closer: back, in fact, to the issue of the white thing in Oslo.

That an icon such as London's Battersea power station can invoke such emotional attachment is quite surprising and difficult to explain for the architect who enjoys sophisticated urban games. It was built almost too late to be really valid as a piece of technology, in a recherché manner and on a Brobdingnagian scale. There is no immediate reciprocator to any signal that it might send. It is surrounded by a sea of scrappy clumps of building in all directions, sitting as an iconic island and raising the question of whether or not any similarly large structure of coherent style would anyhow have the same impact, isolation, or public sympathy. The HOLLYWOOD sign in Los Angeles proves, of course, that the nature of the thing has little to do with the issue. Freestanding letters are enough. If you tell it long enough *it is*. Returning for a moment to Edinburgh or Helsinki, we recall that even the shadowy presence of a heroic profile can sometimes be enough.

Yet when a series of icons can be intelligently posed in key positions of direction and space, the result is so coherent in itself that the architecture (or certainly the architecture between) doesn't really need to be very good. Around the 1890s and early 1900s the edges of the canal system at Gothenburg were articulated by a series of corner turrets that occurred at the change points of the geometry, effectively marking the end of each vista. Walking along, you must wait until you are almost at this corner point before you can read the next run—and of course the next turret at its end. Each turret is related to a sufficiently original facade, so that within a day you can readily identify where you are.

Here we have both coordination and latitude that work together, without any embarrassment about the use of style or form. Critical, of course, is the use of commonality. All the Gothenburg turrets are designed within a certain general aesthetic, accommodating shifts in scale, shape, color, or surface. As do those domed chapels in Moscow and the fluted spires in Copenhagen.

Los Angeles outcrops.

Chrysler Building, New York (William Van Alen).

"New York" pastiche, Las Vegas.

A Reinterpretation of Cluster City

Alison and Peter Smithson coined the term *Cluster City* in the 1950s; in their words, it is "a close knit, complicated, often moving aggregation, but an aggregation with a distinct structure . . . [that] implies that there is not one centre but many." Once understood and inevitably borrowed, it is such a clear objective that I now wonder how I was ever able to stagger around any city without it sitting in my mind. Even in the most endless Tokyo, Melbourne, or Chicago suburb, the memory of it (as an idea) suggests itself, as the mirage of an oasis does in a desert. One looks across urbanized horizons, grasping at straws, gasping for signals.

Seen from the San Diego freeway, the outcropping of Westwood corner, Beverly Hills, and then downtown Los Angeles contain no gems but certainly articulate the north-south line of that city, as do the Midtown and Downtown upsurges of Manhattan. Mass becomes icon. An urban shout perhaps? Bunching the action together, and one wonders if there could be analogies at a more local level.

The detailed interpretation of buildings has certainly incorporated "bunching," especially during periods when quotation of themes has been acceptable. You only have to look dispassionately at American office blocks at any time between the 1900s and 1960s and measure the message-sending content of any ten-foot square. Message content is highest at the peak, diminishing but supportive of the main message down for a few floors. Then a more bland and repetitive offering of windows for many, many floors down until about the third or fourth floor. Then an upswing in iconography and a very articulate set of messages around the lobby levels, and high hype around the entrance. I have not mentioned (you will note) whether this is interpreted through one mannerism or the next. The point is that such architecture knows its priorities just as well as the page layout of a tabloid newspaper does.

Signaling across a suburb or across the pure sheets of a truly Modernist building is a more subtle game. The suburb will accept variation and interference by trees (its charm, as we saw in Chapter 6). It will also accept the placement of reassuring icons at a distance: the church, the bank, the station. But beware the arrogance of large-scale overarticulation, when the social democracy of the suburb is immediately threatened. This same democracy is latent in the discipline of the Modernist aesthetic. Not only is the back (if there is one) admitted to the same status as the front, so the canopy is admitted to the same purity as the roof, the window to the same abstraction as the door, and so on. For one element to send out dizzy signals threatens the clarity of the whole. Yet in all this the art of composition somehow survives. Indeed, composition under all these circumstances is called upon to be very aware of the slightest nuance. The hierarchies and procedures through a cleverly planned suburb are recognizable: the avenue turns and you know (you just know) that the park and lake will reveal themselves. Beyond the bank is the post office. In the same way, there is no doubt where to enter the white cube or which corner houses the director's office.

In my own work, I have been simultaneously fascinated by calmness, sameness, and the distortion of calmness and sameness, more and more until these qualities are exposed as being akin to flaccidity. Just as we get used to the long street and the silent, unremitting steel-paneled walls in the **Arcadia City**, the little rooftop incursions (mere trivia in the first instance) become more and more demonstrative as we walk along the street and eventually take over as *the architecture*.

In the **Finchley Road** project, the weaving metal grids are sufficient presence, but once you stop and peer around, you almost know that one of those strange orange snakes is going to leap out at you. In the **Hamburg Offices** project, Christine Hawley and I enjoyed the spookiness of the fattened and curled end of the building that belied the well-mannered behavior of both of the long sides. Strangely enough, this spooky end had much to say up close to the adjoining and rather Gothic building, thus letting the rhetoric of the main form talk to the river and to the long view in a manner that was far more languid and wry.

Here and there in one's travels, there is the opportunity for a conglomeration of large buildings to talk to each other and still present a collective power that sends signals to the city as a whole. The parts of Edinburgh castle do this, as does the Potola at Lhasa, Mies van der Rohe's Lake Shore Drive apartments in Chicago, or (seen at certain angles) the identifiable terraces up on the hills at Bath. In each of these examples, the shared languages have different tones and pitches, but they inform the city, giving it identity and purpose.

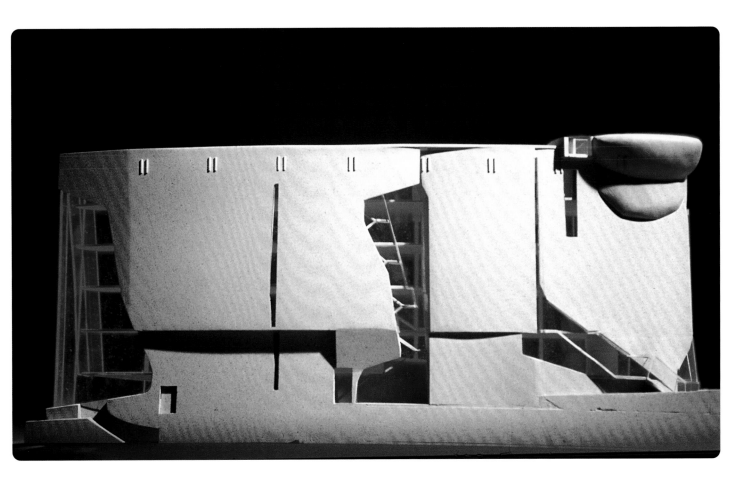

Very Pleased

Before reaching any conclusion about the rhetoric of cities or the consciousness of rhetorical elements, I pause in the face of those cities that are so self-satisfied with their own hierarchy of signaling that, to me, they destroy the architectural climate. Indeed, for whatever reason, they are conspicuous in their effective castration of new architecture.

In Prague, there is much admiration of the set pieces that perch on the hillsides above the Vltava or relax on its embankments. It is picturesque, binding, and immensely pleased with itself. Not nearly as pleased, however, as is the city of Jerusalem, loaded and pummeled by the insistence of at least three major religions and as many millennia that it is a *significant place*. The results are to be found in a collection of architecture that is (when viewed objectively) rather poor. Curious, isn't it, that all this concern, all this history, all this interpretation, angst, layering, reinterpretation (not to mention the neat, quartermaster's psychology of the 1920s to 1950s that insisted on "stone—but only stone") could seem only to stultify the creative juices of so many builders? Given the hornet's nest of the Old City, the rest has never recovered its equilibrium. It is, for me, the most tragic city that I know—which is easy to say—but also the most irritating city that I know—which is more difficult to say. Deep down, my irritation is connected to my cultural need for relaxedness, for freedom of initiative, for the freedom to whistle as you walk, sing a new tune, wink at the jokers, put up two fingers at the pompous. None of which would go down very well in such a paranoid place. So it is almost a self-fulfilling irony that recent buildings seem to be made of a scaled-up version of those shortbread biscuits that you dip into a cup of tea. No dipping allowed here, of course.

In order to speak, architecture needs freedom.

Grand Canal, Venice.

Edinburgh, which is also pleased with itself, is saved by spatiality, mists, and a sufficient touch of the Gothic to harbor the gremlins.

Rome, also a pompous place, is saved by having a few knockout punches that bully out the potential drone of self-importance of the rest. You can't argue with an oval colonnade that has not only survived twenty centuries but still looks impressive and ready for action. You can't argue with an enormous cathedral that stretches out a pair of crab claws sufficient (at least architecturally) to seduce even the most hardened nonbeliever. And with the Pantheon, we bow to the audacity of a massive dome with the provocation of its open eye.

So it is left for Venice, that most pleased with itself of all, to challenge the contemporary architect on the subject of values, operations, form, and the longevity of any symbolism related to such things. Such is its power as a placebo, such is its irritating *niceness* that we are encouraged to forget that it was created as a tough, functional, opportunist base for scavengers (which generated the manipulations of water, wall, orifice, or gadget) and that these things directly created the formal tapestry and picturesque atmosphere that tourists delight in. The studied management of its assumed gentility is such that it offers a little bit of "culture" at every turn. A mannered Muzak. A cloying preciousness and a do-not-touch response to the modern parallels of that same opportunism that would have been involved in its premummified lifetime.

Ironically, some city designers crave to discover the jungle-juice that can reproduce such a wonderful place. They reproduce the tapestry, they keep the music sweet like the elevator Muzak that you just recognize as Beethoven with the loud bits orchestrated out. The "New Urbanism" is a typical result: manageable and soothing. Fortunately, there are enough cities of strong iconography and clusters waiting to coagulate.

O.T.T.

Larger cities are able to take violent punches. They drift and sag, they change internal patterns of allegiance. They dream up places of significance, often without the help of architects. Indeed, by the time architects become involved, the motivation has started to run down and the action has probably moved elsewhere.

In the 1960s and 1970s architects became uneasy about their ability to affect the city as it is experienced. No doubt, Postmodernism was one response. Regionalism another. Some European architects looked at a hitherto ignored world that simultaneously attracted the attention of the more lively American and English artists: pop in music, in art, in photography linked through to a parallel recognition of the strength of the collage. Not just as an escape from the still life and the picture frame but from set hierarchies and procedures in all things. We looked at the shantytowns on the English coast. We looked at sheds in the garden and at rubbish in waste bins. We photographed the American strips: the looser and tackier, the better. We collected shots of what later became known as Googie architecture. Eduardo Paolozzi's collages reminded us of the connection between Donald Duck, an India rubber cactus, and the lighter-than-air machine as aspects of twentieth-century culture that were every bit as significant as the link between Braque, Le Corbusier, and the deep Mediterranean shadow.

Reyner Banham's ability to draw significance from the everyday—whether a burger bar, an Italian scooter, or a bloke in a hat—was found to be based upon continuous reference back to the theoretical base of Modernism.

Out of these influences, as well as the living example of Buckminster Fuller as the high priest of action and invention, came the work of Archigram. So you can find a particular moment—exactly the winter of 1968–69 when I sat in Los Angeles making my own version of Instant City, to be sited in an English field but already confirming the existence of that

The Camden Lock phenomenon, London, 2001.

The Camden Lock phenomenon, London, 2001.

The Ginza area at night, Tokyo.

other, looser iconography existing just down the street. Made of signs and giant swathes of colored surface, traipsed across by wires and cracks but in full power of impact nonetheless. The circus, the seaside, and the Californian strip were, for me, *the same thing*.

Neat technology is wonderful: my friends at the Foster office leapt with joy when they achieved *the world's longest neoprene strip* at the Sainsbury Centre in Norwich during the 1980s. Yet it cannot communicate its wonder. A shape and a winking light *can*. Here lies the dilemma.

The most hilarious running experience, two kilometers from home, is the transformation of Camden Town into a zany version of such a strip. Who would have believed that a very seedy (but intact) piece of London with some hard streaks of raised railway and a slimy canal could become a totally over-the-top pop art strip? Itsuko Hasegawa, one of the most fearless users of formal icons that I know, had it in a flash: "It's not England—it's Los Angeles." Of course, not the Los Angeles of now, but a bulbous, slightly crafted extension of the old strip advertising attached by big rusting bolts to London stock brick facades. The real explanation is complex: it has to do with London as a tourist trap and the charm of the slimy canal when commercialized. The issue here is what, if anything, it can offer the current generation of architects, once again uneasy about their ability to affect the experience of the city. Or what it offers me? Does it suggest that distortion of scale, quotation, and graphic superimposition have a legitimate place in the making of a city? We know something of this from the "Photoshop revolution" with its facility for mixing scales. The openness of juxtapositions; the role of grid, scale, or discipline from which we take off into a rapid redeployment. As the edifice rushes across space, as the collection of references becomes more and more acquisitive, there comes the need for the occasional signal *that is very obvious*.

Looking at and Looking out

At **St. John's Wood** I reckoned upon an ideal place to experiment with the notion of looking out as the generator of a building, with views across Regent's Park and the center of London as a skyline. As always, I was fascinated by the abilities of screens and filtering meshes, but now it was possible to incorporate the abilities of smart glass and of the superimposition of liquid-crystal imagery onto the *actual window*. The window need no longer remain a mute skin held in a hole in the wall.

The window could be programmed and the view through it could be:

(1) a simple view through the park

(2) an electronically enhanced view through the park

(3) a superimposition of Granny's cottage onto the view

(4) the current stock-market prices

(5) a Hawaiian sunset

(6) any mix of 1 to 5

The possibilities are endless. It could have just rested there, but I felt the need to celebrate the emancipation of the window. I developed the "eyelash" element. Indeed, the rhetoric of the building depends on these circular eyelashes to tell the world that this building is about *looking*. Its mannerisms are quite expressionistic and refer back to the world of individual statement in which each dwelling tells you it is there; the eyelashes move and reveal that sometimes parts of the building are asleep.

To respond to the city of Tel Aviv is a more demanding task. For one thing, it is rarely asleep. For another, there is no delicate park or romantic old skyline. There is some raunchy old cement work at ground level and a scatter of towers—as yet without a cluster. You can insert any structure into this and you will be considered a wimp if you don't assert yourself. Moreover, the city is a celebration of opportunism. A city of the deal, the angle, a city of endless conversation. So my group of **towers for the Medina Circle** is the product of an Englishman wanting desperately to join in this babble. The site has a highly legitimate origin, however. Oscar Niemeyer created the concept for this circular parade for the bourgeoisie of the north end of the city. He instigated (though not in detail) the mannerism of the segments of the buildings that ring the circle, whereby they set *back inward*. He intended that there should be three towers in the center, but so far they have not been built. Smart boutiques run round at ground level, but the atmosphere remains a bit dead. You leave the BMW, buy an overpriced cashmere sweater, then drive away.

ST. JOHN'S WOOD HOUSING, detail elevation.
(Peter Cook, 1997)

I jumped into the hiatus, having decided that *my* three towers would be blunt: one for trade, one for parking cars, and one for highly priced apartments. No messing about! The trade tower was the key to it all. In Allenby Street (the old tacky high street of the 1920s, from which Medina has psychologically detached itself), the variety of enterprises is both exotic and (often) a triumph of optimism over economics. In London's Camden "if it don't go—*you* go." But here you need to establish your presence vehemently alongside fellow entrepreneurs and make a sophisticated pitch for yourself. Create showrooms where visitors will stay for an hour, and one in four of them will buy—and buy *big!* Create consultancy suites that are pitched somewhere between a clinic, an agency, and a studio, where psychology and ritual yield as much or more than a straight transaction—this seems absolutely right for the clientele of north Tel Aviv. Not so different from the pitch of the **Finchley Road** project, but set up in the air. A good mix can be with clubs and short-stay hotels. Another mix being rent-by-the-day offices. Health clubs, a TV station. Furniture displays. Small-scale exhibition events. Some conferencing.

So make it a sandwich. A club sandwich with each typological layer articulating itself. But keep the car park simple, with a mechanized plug-in parking system clothed in a mesh skin upon which vegetation is encouraged to grow as fast as possible. Keep the housing as simple as possible: clearly for singles and doubles with a one-minute-to-the-car psychology. In retrospect, a cluster, but also a return to uninhibited expression. A building unashamed of stating its game.

At the other end of the city, near old Jaffo, I propose an opposite strategy. A single mode of expression. A closed world. Half the year it is hot and humid. The city is noisy and often troubled. So this tower can be an escape—almost in the nature of the hovering airship. A place in which technology and an irreverent response to the local day cycle can be manipulated. The circular plan is wrapped in five layers of skin, the four inner layers being adjustable. The lowest layer is held away from the ground and the world outside. The parking machine is underground.

Several companies rent large volumes and the interior can develop "in-skins" with individual mannerisms or characteristics similar to the circular layers. As in Richard Rogers's Lloyds building, the visitor can get a distant impression of activity and yet concentrate on a locale that feels like a unique space. The Jaffo tower has an inhabited atrium and a mysterious atmosphere created by the technologized veils. Again, as in St. John's Wood, the temptation would be to digitalize the screens.

My response to this city seems to demand both of these contradictory towers: converse reactions exposing the polarities of debate in my mind about the issue of rhetoric. To return to the Smithsons, for whom "Without Rhetoric" became a dictum, I can only reply that without urban rhetoric, the world has so often been inhabited by reiterated mannerism.

TOWER FOR MEDINA CIRCLE, TEL AVIV
(Peter Cook, 1997)

TOWER FOR JAFFO CORNER, TEL AVIV
(Peter Cook, 1997)

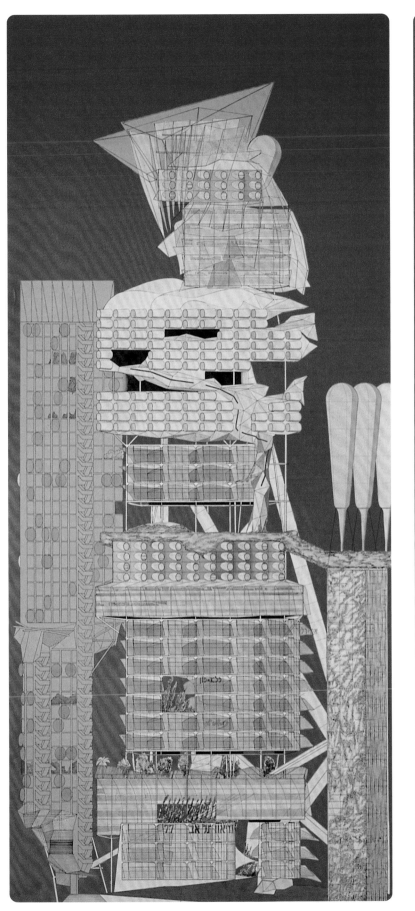
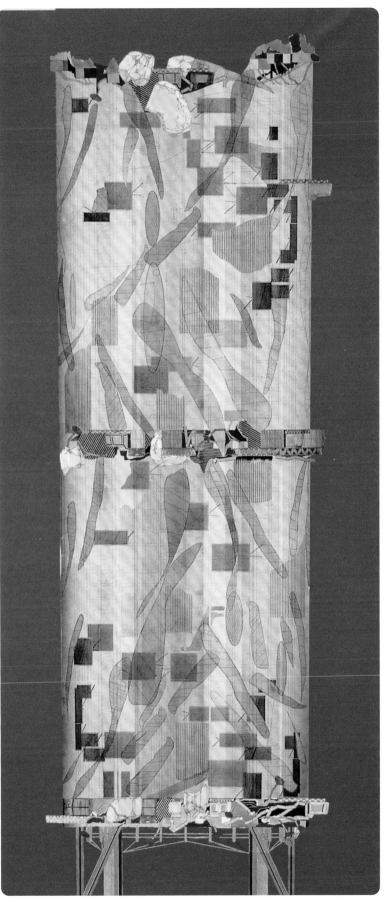

Across Two Thousand Years

There is a certain irony for a futurist-optimist in the successive winning of competitions for museums. A particular irony in directly responding to a world that existed two thousand years before you—and under your very feet. At **Bad Deutsches Altenberg** (sixty kilometers east of Vienna), Christine Hawley and I deliberately kept the scale of our buildings small, not just in volume (as they had to be anyway) but consciously inserted into the ground as a series of fragments.

At that place was the Roman city and fortress of Carnuntum. Our site, the **Pfaffenberg** hillside, is strewn with rocks and a seemingly endless yield of Roman artifacts. The task was to infiltrate it by extending the museum and then making a pavilion, a belvedere, and an open-air theater up in the undergrowth. Intriguingly, two other icons already existed on the site: a so-called Turkish burial mound at the highest point and a rather good (and rather eclectic) Gothic church.

MUSEUM OF ANTIQUITIES, PFAFFENBERG
Network of elements.
(Peter Cook and Christine Hawley, 1996–)

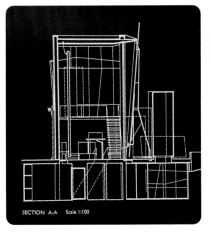

MUSEUM OF ANTIQUITIES, PFAFFENBERG. Section.

SECTION A-A   Scale 1:100

MUSEUM EXTENSION:
STREET ELEVATION   Scale 1:100

main Museum

MUSEUM OF ANTIQUITIES, PFAFFENBERG. Elevation.

MUSEUM OF ANTIQUITIES, PFAFFENBERG. Open-air theater, elevations.

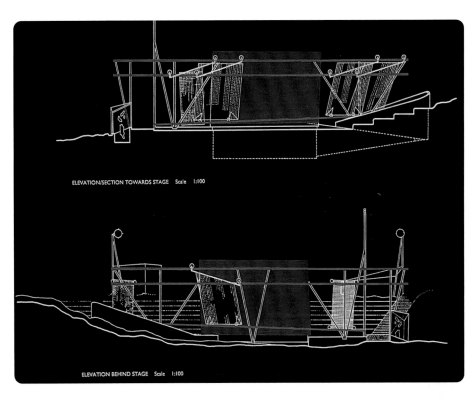

ELEVATION/SECTION TOWARDS STAGE   Scale 1:100

ELEVATION BEHIND STAGE   Scale 1:100

MUSEUM OF ANTIQUITIES, PFAFFENBERG. Pavilion, section.

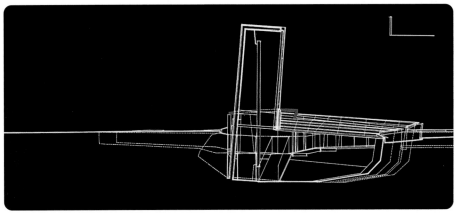

In the midst of this designated area for relaxation, just up from the spa, close to the Danube, with dense trees and gentle clearings, there were surely ghosts. The very information and relics that we were to house would accumulate and add weight to the evidence that a busier and more articulate dynamic had once held sway among these same rocks. Aggression and enterprise were being remembered and celebrated. At all costs we had to avoid the cloying sentimentality of making neo-Roman. We had to avoid Swiss piety. We had to make machines to summon back those ghosts.

What was needed was a series of foils to the fragments—not necessarily buildings but armatures and screens that could intrigue a languid public and protect outcrops that could appear out of the ground and continue to sustain their interest as they moved closer. A vocabulary of simple screens, small cages, and a hybrid of display case and miniature pavilion emerged from the study. We would extend the museum with a large room that could flap out and run under the earth, meandering around the rocks and spurting up through the garden at many points with relics at each point. A ramped path, emanating from the room, would then begin to zigzag around the garden. The front of the room (facing the street) is in the form of a calm steel shield. Slim and lyrical elements—the frames, the armatures, and the handrails are also in steel. They do not compete with the chunks of stone as they articulate and identify the small fragments.

Up on the hill is the open-air theater. A piece of simple land carving with a stage and backdrop that are tuned and mechanized. The backdrop itself is (again) a calm steel shield, slightly tilted from the vertical. There is also the occasional glass outcrop with its relic on this site.

Further up the hill is the exhibition pavilion, tucked discreetly into the ground but with one tall slit of space that sits above a twist in the path linking the pavilion with the rest of the ensemble. The slit is the third steel shield, and it tilts even more off the vertical. The room itself is dug into the ground and its glass roof can be walked over. Within lies the large model of Carnuntum as it would have been.

On the top of the cliff, overlooking the museum, sits the final new element: the belvedere. Our instruction was to avoid digging for more than a few centimeters into the ground since it is riddled with relics. The steel shield now lies horizontally—as a reference, as a raft, as a final statement of articulation and protection. The steel armatures become their most lyrical on this site, making further comment about interchange between places of like manner, separated by space.

Each site speaks to the next, not only by the reuse of elements and their mannerisms, but also by a deliberate setting up of antennae—paths, gantries, screens—where appropriate, in a direct line. Moreover, the church and the mound are brought into the system. What we have is a series of Cook-Hawley lay-lines encouraging the buildings to ricochet from each other. The six points are the generators of signals so that the coverage of the territory is not a "city" in the built-up sense, and the former city is invisible. Yet the field is doubly charged and we are quite conscious of making signals.

In support of the iconic I have therefore darted back from the hot to the cool, the arrogant to the humble, the popular to the tectonic. From cities I love or cities I despise to noncity cities. This business of expression is scary but tantalizing and we are only just beginning to tackle it. So far, I continue to believe that our available languages of architecture are too few and our willingness to mix them is too feeble.

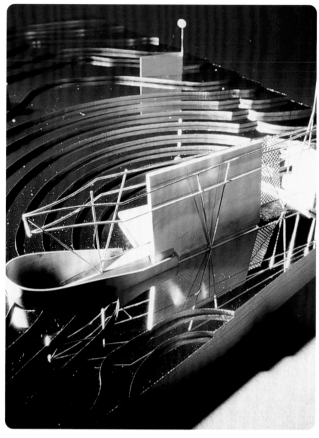

MUSEUM OF ANTIQUITIES, PFAFFENBERG. Open-air theater, model.

MUSEUM OF ANTIQUITIES, PFAFFENBERG. Belevedere, model.

THE CITY UNDER THE TREES

Super-Houston

Strange that Super-Houston is the one scheme that has been born directly out of an academic base. Over many years of teaching I have been consciously reluctant to force a piece of design out of the formality of the seminar or the studio program (except for the Brisbane Towers, which only used the same site as the students and not much more).

I had already spent a few days in Houston here and there and had benefited from Reyner Banham's frequent observations and inevitable comparisons with Los Angeles. I had sweated my way across a campus in the heat and stickiness of September. I had dashed for air-conditioned cover in a car or lobby and then shivered with cold. I had been guided elegantly and amusingly by Stephen Fox through the glades of River Oaks or across into Pasadena, following one's nose as it became more and more aware of the cloying presence of oil in the air. I had walked purposefully down avenues, as a good European, in search of a drugstore; having been told, "It's just a few blocks," I found that it was a sweaty two miles. I had wallowed in the very calmness of the enclave that surrounds Renzo Piano's Menil Museum. I had lined my eye up onto Carlo Jiminez's miniature sets of related pavilions and paths of recognition by which he determined his small house pavilions. In other words, despite the seeming endlessness of Houston, there could be sweet moments, but fazed by the apparent lack of *sequence* in the urban experience.

My task was to conduct morning seminars on a loose series of topics and to respond to Rice's articulate graduate students who had already rumbled by attraction to Los Angeles. Moreover, the architecture school of Rice University was heavily infused with persuasive talent that had moved over from California: Lars Lerup, Albert Pope, and their followers who found themselves making constant reference back and forth from the features of Houston to those of the San Fernando Valley, Orange County, and Beverly Hills, as had Reyner Banham before them. "So, Mr Cook, how do *you* regard the two cities?" My response was instinctive:

To really place Houston, you have to construct a chain of inspirational models. Let's say:

(1) the Italian hill town

(2) London

(3) Los Angeles

(4) Houston . . . and then conjecture something beyond that, with the same level of contradiction . . . let's say

(5) Super-Houston . . .

and I became stuck on the idea for a good two years.

The chain is a personal one, for the Italian hill town had been the love for many of my teachers' generation and for some older English friends, and therefore existed as an irritation as well as an objective model. London was there as my daily reminder that cities are circumstantial and paradoxical—and certainly not all that they seem. Los Angeles had

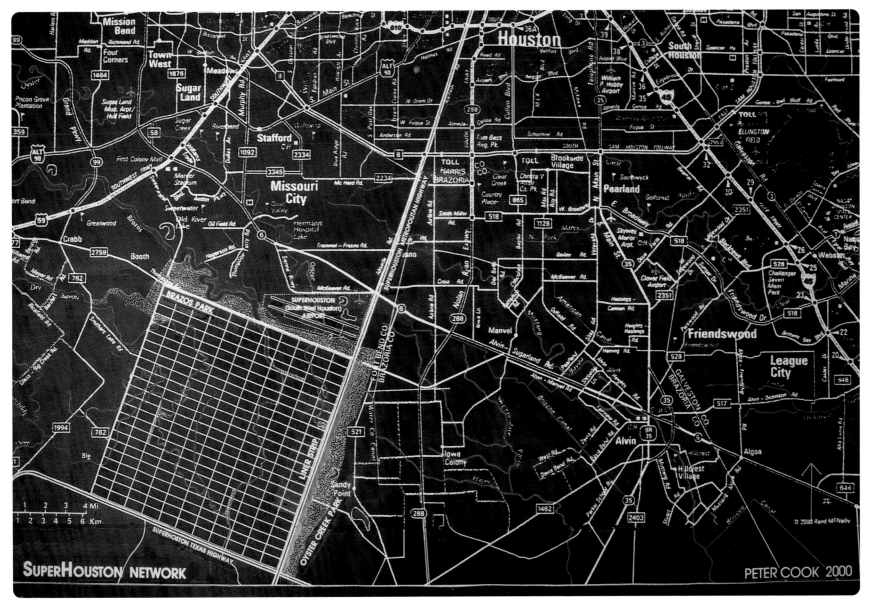

SUPER-HOUSTON, map.

Houston trees, seen from the Warwick Hotel.

Houston within the trees.

Houston under the trees.

remained my running dream, temptation, and revelation, for so much of its sociology is reminiscent of London and even of the British suburban world. Yet its endless provocation of Dream—denial of the Dream—Dream again, kept one on one's intellectual toes. But then Houston? Surely challenging one to delve, to seep into the simultaneous and languid acceptance of both fate and terror suggested by those ambiguous Larry McMurtry characters. A major challenge to spot the most subtle of variations of detail, of nuances, of hints.

In a drive down Westheimer one comes upon the first cluster of outlets—maybe a Burger King, a Walgreens, a Buy-Rite—arranged just clear of the highway and given the usual appliqué styling. Three miles further on, the next cluster of Burger King, Walgreens, but Buy-Rite possibly replaced by a 7-Eleven. Three miles further and the King has moved a few jumps down in the strip, Walgreens is still there and Buy-Rite has reappeared. The architecture (for that is what it must be, must it not, since there are pilasters, corners, and well-mannered edges?) has subtly evolved. They are rarely repeat buildings and the arrangements are particular. But the themes go on. The presence of trees with housing peeking out beneath is as subtle in its conscious market appeal as are the details of the shops. It lacks the layered quality of Los Angeles; it has far fewer remnants of the 1930s, 1940s, or 1950s Googie architecture and even fewer remnants of old enterprise.

In all of this I exclude downtown, for the Houston that fascinates me is the *treed* city. By which I mean the half of the urbanized area where almost continuous tree cover does not prevent a continuity of two-story buildings.

Anyhow, downtown is determined to provide corporate identity and cultural identity markers: the opera, the symphony, and many world headquarters. Yet its rival, the Galleria, is more fascinating, for it acts as a mall (and an unusually long one at that) and as a magnet. It has drawn a cluster of other enterprises around it, rather like a downtown would have done in the 1920s. It has nearly enough variety within it to act as a "city," but not *quite* enough, and this remained in my mind as a working reference when I came to develop the **Liner** element of Super-Houston.

Returning to London between two spells of Rice seminars, I knew that I had to creatively get in there and draw this *Super*-Houston. I was inspired as much by the puzzlement and dismay that had set upon me when, having enjoyed a good haircut, I could not just stroll down the strip beyond the hairdressers: there wasn't one. After a long browse in one of Houston's excellent bookstores I couldn't just mosey over to the record store or even a candy store or even . . . *it just wasn't there*. Even restaurant patterns could be confusing: a well-located but overpopular coffee shop could leave you stranded, as there was no rival or clone across the way, as in other cities. Rice Village excepted, you had to *know* and you had to network.

So there were two experiences running around in my mind: tree cover and scattered networking. Plus the inevitability of the car: not the staccato pattern of dash-and-weave that we have in most other cities. More a *knowing glide* that makes physical the pleasantries of much Texan conversation. It intrigued me too much to let it go.

The Network

Super-Houston must start from the traffic network and a positive attitude toward it. It must offer the ultimate in added value and take the last ounce of strain out of traveling. So why not bug the streets with induction and monitoring electronics? Fit a small device to every local car (and have them available to rent at the edge of town), so that you can let the steering go on automatic pilot. You can dial for a morning's run: "kids," "school," "groceries," "nail bar," "therapist," "Uncle Joe" . . . the network of streets is in a series of one-way routings. Arriving at the school, you would have a reminder signal for waves and pleasantries. Arriving at the grocery store, you silently and uninvolvedly gain a parking slot, similarly for the nail bar and therapist (you don't want him to watch you neurotically fidgeting the car into place, do you?). But for Uncle Joe, there is a half-minute warning signal so that you can get in the mood: do the old traditional drive-up, window down, *wave-and-holler* arrival.

Alternating with the driving streets are an equal number of pathways for the encouragement of jogs, early-morning and evening walking, and small-scale ball games: not all exercise needs a gym. These pathways are of course a rerun of the swathes in the **Layer City** and a memory of the Arcadian atmosphere that can be created beneath good tree cover and among hedges.

At greater intervals, somewhere between a kilometer and a mile, there have to be larger gatherings of through-routes, and at an even larger interval the equivalent of freeways with combinations of guided and unguided tracks. As the scheme developed, it suggested that a ten-mile square of Super-Houston could straddle the low hills and rivulets at the southwestern edge of the existing city.

Over these ten miles we can enjoy something similar in atmosphere to McMurtry's description of "the well-tamed forests of River Oaks." Swathes of trees and clearings, an even spread of middle-income houses, and some slightly more show-off houses in among them. Small watercourses snaking their way through, but not sufficiently grand or constant to cause any ceremony or interruption in the general spread. Similarly, there needs to be some occasional splitting open of the run of building, enough to host a public park or playing fields, but definitely nothing too special. The establishment of an evenness greater than that of Houston itself sets up the ultimate tease: to determine event where there is none. To proliferate the *same* and then invite the inhabitant to suss out the *particular*. You can always find the particular in the Yellow Pages or on the Internet—if you know what you are looking for. And even if you don't—you can get a vicarious urge to do something, visit something or someone, buy something by scanning down through these seemingly bland sources of information.

To someone who, in the preceding pages, has surely exposed himself as a place-inspired, thing-inspired, event-inspired designer, this pursuit of the bland can be recognized as a self-tease but also a conscious exercise in reassembling the criteria of action. The temporary detachment of mannerism from event is stimulating and intriguing. Centuries of conscious and physical celebration—of looking, stopping, starting, worshiping, selling, or even just passing over a river—have given architects the excuse to articulate day-to-day life and freeze the values of a monarchy or a civilization in stone.

And anyway, what the hell?

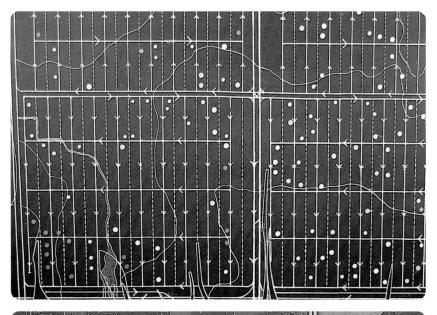

SUPER-HOUSTON, network.

SUPER-HOUSTON, network and trees.

SUPER-HOUSTON, locality plan.

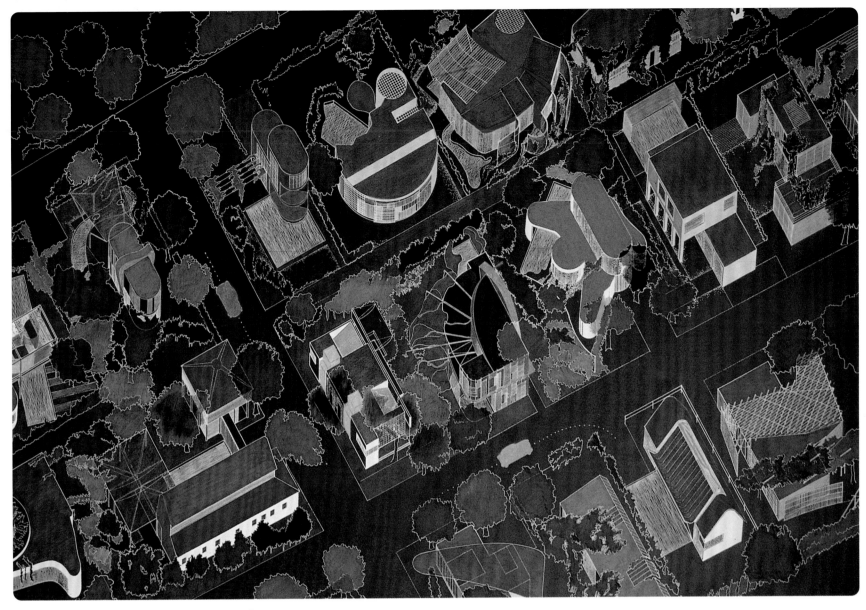

SUPER-HOUSTON, typical housing, axonometric.

The Carpet

At another level, the fascination for endless suburbia could be a resigned (or cynical?) commentary on the feebleness of architectural values, on the fickleness of the public, on the skin-deep quality of "styling," on the ultimate exchangeability of it all. Or it can be a deliberate inversion of one's normal procedure of sniffing the air, searching for clues, erecting a system of values, and then—and only then—making some moves toward design and its expression. A holiday from sensitivity? A vacation from Europe and all its ghosts?

The only ghosts under these trees are surely to be found inside the houses themselves. But then the fun starts. If the proposition included the idea that there need not be any particular typology for houses, there similarly need not be any typology for restaurants, either (a popular Houston eatery is already called the House). How different is a consultancy from an office or from a soft-sell specialist shop or from a small church? How different is a house with a mail-order business in the garage from a house with a boat in the garage? For years in England we have had a detached or even anarchic attitude toward the mainland European penchant for the typological. We love stories of the man in north London's Edgware with a full-sized Wurlitzer organ in his front room, the enterprising Greek in south London's Clapham who runs a fish-and-chip shop round at the side door of a normal house, or the guy who . . . and as the stories proliferate they give us great satisfaction that all those ordered and logical plans based upon optimized behavior and all that clean *Dutchness* can't keep a good anarchic tradition down!

The refusal of the true Middle American to be totally tied down in his or her private life is a strong motivation to the designer of a Super-Houston. But one has to be careful in admitting this. Conversations with Americans can lead you into unexpected traps. The European can mistakenly read the offering of intimate personal details as openness, not realizing that there is still a code of concealment involved. Now turn this over into the design of a house. The bourgeois nature of Houston and a big chunk of the city is just that, suggesting that people still only want to display a certain status and few selected clues out onto the street.

Driving in Super-Houston, you may now glide along with the release of time and mental concentration and *may be* transferred toward the crossword puzzle or game of cards with your passenger. But you also have more time to poke your eye around the neighborhood. What part of the activity within could be transferred out onto the street? Does the podiatrist's clinic act as a cottage, the fire station as a museum, the family house as an aquarium? You can invent endless pairings. There is no longer any functionalist ethic. No one-to-one correspondence left.

Of course, the truth is that I could not resist some essays in interpretation. I took the proposition down to the scale of house shapes to the on-plot shapes: some bending and flexing toward a watercourse and even the odd break with my own rules so that a small supermarket could violate the even texture of small buildings. I continued and suggested occasional house types so that I could respond to the climate of a place that surely does not have to consist of air-conditioned boxes and deserted porches. The question of privacy, too, engaged me because it seems so ambiguous in the American psychology. In one house I designed a series of walls running out from the private bedroom of each member of the family so that each would have a private garden. If they wanted, they could run straight from the shower through the room and out onto a lawn with no clothes on—enjoying the sweet damp of it all!

I enjoy the provocation of curled, curved, and lyrical forms in among a scenery that *one knows* will be predominantly orthogonal. One tries to be styleless and guileless, but at the same time one has to recognize—and probably enjoy—the fact that if Super-Houston is to be more Houston than Houston, its carpet of houses will be highly irritating, bland, low-key, fake, schmockey in every way to the architect of the European salon (not to speak of New York or Los Angeles salons).

I hope that by this point I have built up around this project and my attitude to it a sufficient head of love-hate steam to carry out the ultimate volte-face?

SUPER-HOUSTON, "Yards 2" house, plan.

SUPER-HOUSTON, view to a village along the freeway.

SUPER-HOUSTON, aerial view of the Liner.
(Computer projection by Nicola Haines)

The Liner

It was never enough just to propose this ten-mile carpet of stuff on its own. The edge condition of cities has been a fascination ever since I can remember: the villages that snake out from the edges of the old cities; the pre-car suburbs that carried out their love-hate relationships with mother Metropolis, squeaking about (but not really believing in) their independence and individuality. Now the more recent edges with their sales sheds. Or the town that has to acknowledge another town even if they are spaced apart? What is Brooklyn to Manhattan? Oakland to San Francisco? South London to North London?

Once again, the airport gave me many clues. But to focus on the issue I simultaneously remembered those three great detached-but-unforgettable twentieth-century "ships" of architecture: Le Corbusier's Unité d'habitation sitting on the edge of Marseilles, Hans Hollein's collaged aircraft carrier sitting on the hills of Burgendland, and of course Ron Herron's Walking City, sitting somewhere near where you might want to be.

My only experience of such a phenomenon came from two Atlantic crossings by ocean liner. Indeed, a *city* and, as with the three heroic models, a *selective* city.

So the eastern flank of Super-Houston acquired a ten-mile-long strip of stuff: everything that cannot—or does not want to—be part of the two-story carpet is in this strip. Behind it is the park, also ten miles long. Behind the park is the open countryside. Just as in a liner, there are decks. Just as in a liner, there are endless shifts of function and endless surprises. Just as in a liner, there is a linear arrangement but not an insistent one (of the type that you might have found in a 1960s linear city diagram).

Before this all gets too cozy, we find that the actual arrangements within are more wayward and circumstantial than they would be in the confines of an ocean liner and, anyhow, the whole thing is sixty times longer than any ship would be. As the various activities find their way into the Liner, they establish clumps of logical activity. Some are large (production lines and sales sheds), some are minute (kiosks and bridges). After the relentlessness of the ten-mile square carpet—or do I mean the boringness of it?—there is the picturesque quality of what I am coyly calling *wayward*. I am invoking some instincts about locale together with the particular, the self-focused: all those qualities of the dreaded *Italian hill town*!

During the composition of the Liner, I became acutely aware of the significance of the freeway line sitting between a ten-mile carpet deliberately without focus and a ten-mile-long sliver of circumstantially collaged this-and-that. There was the need to do four things at once:

(1) to give some edge icons for the carpet dwellers

(2) to offer (for once) an opportunity for heroics

(3) to set up a series of foci for the Liner

(4) to give the highway that indexlike quality that I enjoy back on the L.A. freeway.

The design solution was a series of darts, feather-shaped objects with flat sides. Anything from ten to a hundred meters long and of relatively similar height. They slash across the freeway. They sometimes cut into it. They dart—in small, directional clusters—into the Liner. Occasionally they dart the other way and lose themselves in the trees.

As I worked on them, these darts took on more and more overtones. They could be read as giant billboards, bigger and bolder than any on Sunset Boulevard. As such they could acquire or deny as much or as little architectural character as you wished. Ideal in a culture where the boundaries between reality, represented imagery, surface, hypersurface, implicit content, and explicit content are all up for a scramble. Indeed, in a single set of darts there could be various gradations of consistency of content: bland, bland-to-hint, hint, strong hint, icon, shrill icon, dissolve. But all of them pink! The next set, down the road, might be all gridded and shiny but never declaring anything specific, yet still as recognizably dart-shaped as the pink ones.

The role played by the sets of darts brought to mind memories of childhood drives through middle England. Successive glimpses of villages with their particularity marked out by very few elements, but strongly placed, strongly formed, and certainly distinct from each other.

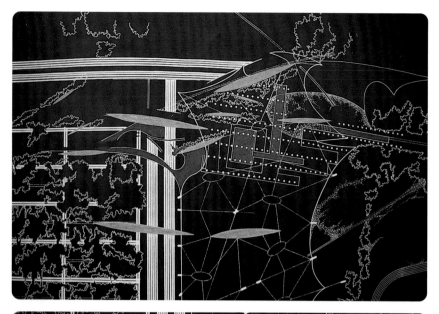

SUPER-HOUSTON, Village 1, plan.

SUPER-HOUSTON, Village 2, plan.

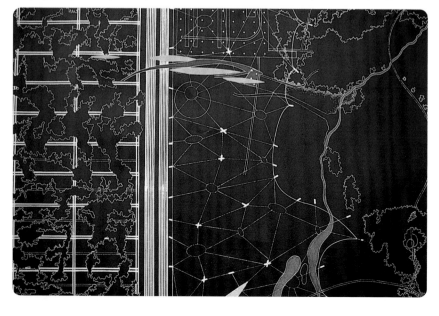

SUPER-HOUSTON, Village 3, plan.

SUPER-HOUSTON, Village 4, plan.

SUPER-HOUSTON, Village 5, plan.

SUPER-HOUSTON, Village 6, plan.

The Villages and the Liner

At the northern end of the strip, the park cuts across, completing the formation of Super-Houston.

Village 1 therefore has a key role to play, the arrival point from older Houston in the north. As it is the start of a run of "villages," there was the temptation is to play it heroic. The darts here are almost certainly hotels, the first patch of Liner a hypermarket of some sort. South of this is a loose stretch of covered territory, cheap enough and accessible enough to attract people from the region. It is a market, coming and going over different days of the week. The whole Liner has three clear floors of parking below and a deliberately gentle and floating tent structure above.

There is no need for the internal "buildings" to get involved with full weatherproofing. Folds in the tent and reflective surfaces are contrived to create cross-breezes and keep the place cool.

Village 2 is deliberately quite modest both in its presence and as an announcement of itself to the freeway (this time the darts only just edge into the line of sight, rather than act as gates). There is a raised platform, like an enclosed village green. Trees pass right across from the carpet of houses, through the Liner, and out into the park at a key point where there is a sports track. Almost symbolically, the Texan forest cuts across to remind us that even the big-scale elements are only here to support the general verdure: not to dominate it.

Yet in the territory leading toward **Village 3**, there is ample reminder of the need for Houston to support itself by serious industrial activity, and the darts at this village can easily house the administration of that activity as well as acting as an enormous signboard for it. Across the freeway there is a generous "swan" of a bridge that leads the jogger or the walker straight over from private lawns to the park and its small river: no need to engage in trade or noise.

Village 4 can be more exotic. By now some three miles away from the northern corner, it sets up a cluster of platforms and enclosures that might have the rhetoric and competitiveness of a traditional town. There are only five darts, but they are hotel-sized and bold enough to deposit one of their number into the carpet zone. It is almost certainly a recreation-based village, anticipating the serious activities going on in the next village to the south.

A highly gridded and structured zone contains laboratories, possibly an extension of the Houston Medical Center, and just into the park, more running tracks and playing fields; year-round sports happen under the flanks of the tent system.

So it is left for **Village 5** to restate the idea of a possible countersystem. A giant mile-long footbridge gives an overview to the Liner and (once again) links the housing carpet to the park. Fast, hard slabs of platform shower away from the bridge. This is a village that calls for a definite citywide role: one for the fast and fearless, one for the world of entrepreneurship, perhaps advertising, perhaps laboratories or the entertainment industry. A giant dart caps it all, way out into the park. Yet like any strong city, the general relationship of carpet-highway-liner-park is not seriously threatened, just tweaked and enlivened by this feisty village.

Perhaps **Village 6** is the weirdest one so far, for there are only two darts—none in the carpet zone and a giant one out in the park. Trees (a thick band of them, no less) force their way across the freeway and give as much identity to this moment in the game as would have the toughest of built forms. Small enterprises huddle into the tent: an open-air concert venue and a scooped-out stretch of river occur before the quiet event of **Village 7**.

SUPER-HOUSTON, Villages 7, 8, and 9, plan.

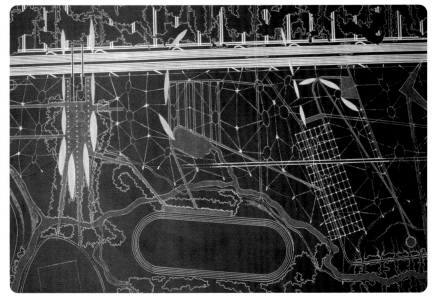

SUPER-HOUSTON, Villages 9, 10, and 11, plan.

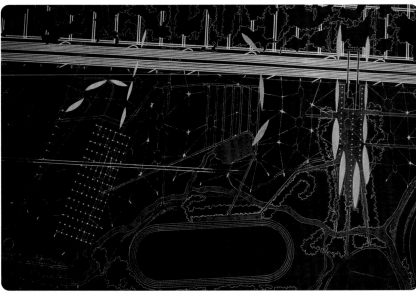

SUPER-HOUSTON, Villages 11, 12, and 13, plan.

Conclusion

It is the commentary of a designer. One can only spend so much time collecting incidents before one needs to splice them together into sets of significance. More dangerously, into patches of theory.

As an architect, one's impulse is to play odd sets of them back into the cities themselves, though they might find themselves going back into the wrong city, and sometimes this can happen with delightful results.

In Super-Houston, my privilege is that of creative indulgence. To treat myself as a piece of intellectual elastic, stretching my tolerance of the mundane and then letting the elastic go with a judder that ricochets right down the Liner, thus exposing so many of my memories and tastes in the medium I most enjoy—the wizzling line.